Organizing for Science in Britain

A case-study

IAN VARCOE

OXFORD UNIVERSITY PRESS 1974

Oxford University Press *Ely House, London, W.I.*

Glasgow	Delhi
New York	Bombay
Toronto	Calcutta
Melbourne	Madras
Wellington	Karachi
Cape Town	Lahore
Ibadan	Dacca
Nairobi	Kuala Lumpur
Dar es Salaam	Singapore
Lusaka	Hong Kong
Addis Ababa	Tokyo

ISBN 0 19 858319 2

© OXFORD UNIVERSITY PRESS 1974

Setting: D. Harvey & Co. Ltd.
Printed in Great Britain by
J. W. Arrowsmith, Bristol

And if one or two have the boldness to use any liberty of judgement, they must undertake the task all by themselves; they can have no advantage from the company of others. And if they can endure this also, they will find their industry and largeness of mind no slight hindrance to their fortune. For the studies of men are confined, and, as it were, imprisoned in the writings of certain authors, from whom if any man dissent he is straightway arraigned as a turbulent person and an innovator... But arts and sciences should be like Mines, where the noise of new works and further advances is heard on every side.

FRANCIS BACON, *The New Organon*

Preface

The research councils are the chief links between the State in its role as performer, promoter (and, more recently, purchaser) of scientific research and the institutions in which the sciences are practised and taught. Yet comparatively little is known about them: their origins and the dilemmas which confront them at various stages of industrial development have not been explored in any systematic way. We lack, too, a knowledge of their impact on scientific research and the response of scientists and practitioners to them, and, less concretely but of pressing concern, their contribution to technological and social change and their role in fostering the spread of scientific ways of thinking. The special position of the Council for Scientific and Industrial Research as the earliest, the largest and most economically important, and, to many, the least successful of the research councils makes it an obvious subject for study with these questions in mind. The availability of archival materials for the period 1916-39 held out the prospect of discovering at least some of the answers to them, answers which, although subject to modification in the event of further documents coming to light, would be more intellectually satisfying than any so far available. Moreover, provided the approach was carefully thought out and was broad in scope, they would, it was felt, not only suggest insights into the broader consequences of the DSIR's existence and operation, but would also afford a basis for assessing both the cultural significance of attempts to stimulate research through government sponsorship and its strengths and weaknesses as a mode of organization. However, even primary sources may be seriously misleading. In particular, they may fail to convey to the student the atmosphere of the organization, that elusive element which is, nevertheless, quintessential to its functioning. I have learnt much in this regard from Sir Harry Melville and from conversations with Lord Kings Norton, Sir Graham Sutherland, and Mr. Henry

Preface

Wooldridge. Thanks are also due to Dr. W.L. Francis of the Science Research Council and to Dr. R.A.E. Galley.

My greatest debt, however, is to Sir Frederick Dainton, who, as Editor of the series, suggested the book and encouraged me during its preparation. Others, who only a sense of what is customary prevents me from acknowledging at greater length, are Mr. D.N. Chester, who has guided my thinking from the beginning, Professor Eric Hutchinson and Dr. Roy Macleod, both of whom were kind enough to comment on an earlier version of Chapter 2, and Professor Max Beloff, who proved to be a truly incisive critic of the whole. None of these people, needless to say, are responsible for any of the study's errors or shortcomings.

Leeds,
November 1972   I.V.

Contents

1 Introduction   1

2 The origins of the DSIR   9

3 The idea of the DSIR   18

4 Co-operative research   23

5 Corporate research   34

6 The organization of government science   44

7 The DSIR and the universities   61

8 Conclusion   75

  Notes and references   85

  Index   91

Introduction

In setting out to reconstruct an institution's development the chronicler is inevitably confronted with a vast amount of information from which he must select. He is, therefore, under an obligation to make explicit the categories which will determine his subject-matter, and to explain why he has adopted this set of categories rather than another. At first sight, the subject of the present study — the Department of Scientific and Industrial Research (DSIR), 1916-64 — would not appear to raise anything other than simple questions of fact. But there will always be as many approaches to a phenomenon as there are presuppositions concerning it, and it matters not only for the initial definition of a field of interest but for subsequent interpretation which of these is chosen. The point of view from which I have approached the DSIR is that of an interest in its contribution to the growth of organized research.

The question immediately arises: is this a category of research in terms of which information can be gathered and ordered in a straightforward way? Unfortunately, this is not the case. Views as to the way of organizing for research which best allows the progress of scientific research and the application of its results not only differ considerably, but some are based on an assessment of what, at least to their authors, appears to have been the experience of bodies engaged in the task, while others are not. It would be inappropriate in the context of these preliminary remarks to trace the history of the debate about what, for want of a better term, can be called the 'Haldane' view of the proper organization of scientific research. Nevertheless, if one is to begin to account for the growth of public and private investment in industrial research since 1914, and the role of the DSIR in promoting the employment of an increasing number of persons in scientific research on a full-time basis, it is not sufficient simply to state that current assessments of the significance of this development and of the conditions under which it has occurred are open to question. It is precisely because they are questioned that it is necessary to guard against misinterpretation in advance by stating precisely what the terms must be taken to mean.

1

A study of the contribution of the DSIR to the institutional development of industrial research involves an examination of the degree to which its activities conformed to certain criteria which came in the late 1950s to be seen as prerequisites of a 'policy' for scientific research. The pace and direction of scientific effort should, it was felt, represent the realization of priorities based on assessments of the likely path of development in various fields. A key role was therefore assigned to advisory bodies devoted to the tasks of relating science to the traditional concerns of policy, organizing research at various levels within the government, and balancing pure and applied research effort.

Of the early bodies formed in response to the need to organize scientific research and development, the Advisory Council of the DSIR was perhaps the most striking example. An attempt was made to incorporate technical consultation into the normal processes of government. Scientific considerations, it was expected, would be infused into decision-making at a high level. Almost immediately, the Advisory Council became the object of the attentions of those who saw it as an institution pre-eminently representative of rational investment in innovation. The question was whether the scientists and industrialists who were drawn into advice-giving would adapt themselves to the political and administrative process, and whether they would successfully allocate resources among the spheres in which science and technology was potentially applicable. Initially, these hopes appeared to be in process of fulfilment. The problem facing the Advisory Council was that of identifying neglected areas of research which appeared to warrant further support. Increasingly, however, the question arose not so much of the determination of potentially fruitful fields of investigation, but of the extent to which the Advisory Council was capable of assessing when a project should be terminated. This shift of emphasis was reflected in the type and amount of criticism that the Advisory Council attracted to itself.

In October 1926, the House of Commons Select Committee on Estimates recommended that a subcommittee of the Committee of Civil Research review the adequacy of the DSIR's machinery for co-ordinating research. The Select Committee subsequently recommended that the National Physical Laboratory (NPL) and the Building Research Station take account of ancillary investigations into roads being carried on by the Ministry of Transport. A similar concern lay behind the investigation carried out by the Estimates Committee in 1957. Having considered the organization of the DSIR, it drew attention to the absence of effective liaison with a number of other departments engaged in both civil and defence research and criticized the DSIR for failing to adopt a sufficiently 'active' role in relation to industry. The select committees, however, found little to lead them to question the viability of the DSIR as the primary government agency for the support of industrial research. This was due, in part, to timing. In 1956 the DSIR Act was passed. The Act incorporated the recommendations of a Committee of Inquiry into the DSIR appointed in April 1955 under the chairmanship of Sir Harry Jephcott. The publication of the Committee's report was timed so that its recommendations could be considered by the government in drafting the proposed DSIR Bill. The Committee's main finding was that the existing central direction of scientific effort and the DSIR's research stations, taken as a whole, was 'inevitably inadequate to secure the most effective use of resources in the national interest'; and that many of the research programmes had become 'too diffuse or too uneven in quality'.[1] As a result of the changes which were made after 1956, the Estimates Committee of 1957 commented, 'many criticisms which might have been levelled against the Department's general organization as lately as November 1957 when the estimate was referred to subcommittee B have been rendered out of date by July 1958'. However, while it was, in fact, the case that there was no necessity for considering these questions, it is arguable that had these developments not taken place the Estimates Committee would have been unlikely, by virtue of its composition and interests, to inquire into the scope and balance of the department's research effort.

Apart from the formal tidying up which was effected by the conversion in 1956 of the Advisory Council into an executive Council for Scientific and Industrial Research (CSIR) on the lines of the Medical Research Council (MRC) and the Agricultural Research Council (ARC), it is doubtful whether any substantial changes were effected in the DSIR's policies and procedures. This fact did not escape critics of government scientific and economic policy to whom the DSIR, because of its concern with the application of scientific knowledge to the problems of administration and with encouraging industry to spend more on research and development, particularly at growth-points in the economy, was a key institution. The critics argued that the 'ivory tower' role of the DSIR's central laboratories did little to foster the dissemination of technical information to other administrative departments. A second widely held view was that the DSIR had shown itself unsuited to taking on the positive responsibilities in the industrial sphere which modern government must assume if it is to give effective direction to scientific research in the civilian field.

Between 1960 and 1964, science became a major political issue.[2] Important points of controversy were the role of the Minister for Science and the scope and limitations of the national research and development system. Both issues were central to the question of priorities in research and the broader problem — stressed by both the major political parties — of integrating science policy and economic policy. There was substantial agreement, too, on the need for reform of the Government's organization for civil research. The Treasury Committee on the subject, appointed by the Conservative government under the chairmanship of Sir Burke Trend, reported in 1963. As well as reviewing the state of government support to the universities, the research councils, and research conducted in government departments, the Committee, in its report published in October 1963,[3] touched on a number of important matters, such as ways to enhance the effectiveness of the office of the Minister for Science, the need for a technical policy committee at Cabinet level, and the future of the National Research Development Corporation (NRDC). On the whole, however, its recommendations were undramatic, even cautious. Its severest criticism was directed against the government's organization for industrial research. In the case of newer developments, it pointed out, no coherent arrangements existed to promote research and development. On the other hand, there were instances where arrangements which had a sound historical origin no longer appeared to correspond with the needs of the modern situation. The most striking example was the Admiralty's continuing responsibility for the Royal Observatory, despite the fact that responsibility for other forms of research in astronomy rested with the DSIR. These circumstances rendered the Advisory Council's tasks especially difficult.

II

Most of the Trend Committee's attention was, however, devoted to demonstrating that the DSIR was unsuited to carrying through a programme of industrial modernization. Of particular concern to the Committee was what appeared to be a generally heavy and wasteful expenditure and the seeming inability of the Advisory Council to control it. Indeed, if there is one unqualified conclusion that emerges in the report it is the inability of the Advisory Council to make wise choices, and the corresponding failure of the pattern of sponsored industrial research to represent a coherent view of its place in the national life.

The Advisory Council's failure to formulate criteria for making choices between different fields of science and technology and to guide ·the path of development of research in sectors of British industry of importance to the economy as a whole, was considered sufficiently serious by the Trend Committee to necessitate its abandonment. However, while the DSIR was to be discontinued, the model of the research council as an institution for guiding research was retained. This concept is endorsed by the Trend Committee. In a key sentence it states that 'this principle has contributed significantly to the . . . ability to promote R and D while simultaneously guaranteeing the scientific judgements involved.' It follows that 'autonomous Research Councils should continue to be responsible for much of the scientific research sponsored by the government'*.

But this is not altogether satisfying. For if the principles laid down by the Haldane Committee on the machinery of government in 1918 are not only to be regarded with unqualified admiration but also accepted as viable for the future, how was it freed of the responsibility for the 'haphazard growth' which the CSIR had been unable to restrain and which was the main object of the Committee's censure? The Committee's conclusion avoided the question of why the CSIR should have attracted more unfavourable criticism than the other research councils.

III

Some guidance is provided by a reading of the report of the Haldane Committee itself. Having considered the experience of the first two years of organized industrial research it recognizes that research does not combine readily with non-scientific activities. There is a danger that results will be overlooked and projects discouraged where their relevance to the tasks of the organization responsible for commissioning the research is not immediately apparent. The problem then, and one to which the research council represents only one of several possible solutions, is whether scientific research can be concentrated in such a way as to minimize the accompanying disadvantage of remoteness from users. Under

* In addition to a new Science Research Council the Trend Committee recommended the creation of a new autonomous Industrial Research and Development Authority... *standing in the same relation to the Minister for Science as the Research Councils'* (p. 53; emphasis supplied).

different historical circumstances, the losses necessarily incurred by this particular form of compromise may come to outweigh the gains — so much so, that ultimately it may be more reasonable to judge the effectiveness of society's organization for research in terms of the extent to which it becomes part of the normal processes of administration, production, and distribution; beleaguered certainly, but not self-conscious. The mere existence of a set of administrative arrangements geared especially to the organization and promotion of research in a particular branch of scientific inquiry is, therefore, no guarantee that the research will express a defensible, consistent set of priorities. What are of crucial importance are the exigencies which confront a 'research council' and which limit or extend the courses of administrative action which are open to it. This can be taken to include not just contingent circumstances, but those conditions within the organization and those accumulated commitments to outside elements which are built up on the basis of adaptation to earlier situations of crisis and threat.

It is advisable, therefore, to avoid preconceived notions as to how the Advisory Council should have acted and to enquire into the conditions under which the members are co-opted and their advice sought. In particular, it is necessary to avoid uncritical acceptance of the idea of the research council as providing either a complete interpretation of the past or a panacea for the future. It is necessary also to examine the degree to which the fact of special responsibility for a broad field of scientific research has given rise to the relation to a ministerial 'overlord' and the diffuse forms of influence within a 'market' of agencies and individuals that one would expect of a body officially designated by that term. For it may be that there are specific aspects of actual situations which provide some explanation for the failure of the Advisory Council to maintain a distinct, and therefore legitimate, role in the division of administrative labour. Only in this way will it be possible to establish whether constitutional arrangements that are far from being inherently conducive to the development of a full and explicit consciousness of the complex relations of interdependence sustained by the research council have not only influenced, but have been influenced by, the growth of partial notions concerning its sphere of influence.

A framework for an analysis of this kind is provided by the concept of sponsorship. Sponsorship is the process whereby resources are provided for the encouragement of an activity which is dependent on close association with organizations other than the sponsor, which also seeks to co-ordinate the activity in question. Sponsorship takes two forms:

The individual pattern: This obtains when support is given by the sponsoring body to individuals who are members or employees of outside organizations. The condition for this pattern of sponsorship is a well-defined community of interest among outside organizations in the advancement of certain fields of scientific activity. The provision of encouragement from a single, independent source merely helps to ensure its continued vigour by protecting it from competition with other more institutionalized activities for a share of the organizations' resources.

The collective pattern: This obtains when it is necessary to create, and foster the creation of, organizations which are responsible for the activity in which the sponsoring body is interested. The authority adopting this approach must itself form units of organization in the interests of the community as a whole. It may also give assistance to units, which, while they enjoy a degree of support, are not fully accepted by organizations concerned with substantive problems. These outside organizations remain in competition with one another in all major respects.

The relations between the organizations whose policies the sponsoring body attempts to influence are therefore of crucial importance. Where there is recognition of interdependence the sponsoring body itself can become the centre of decision-making; and the agents of its programme, individuals and loosely knit teams working in independent organizations. Where such recognition is limited or non-existent, it becomes necessary to establish an intermediate layer of organizations which themselves have sponsoring functions. They attempt to foster awareness of problems, to secure contributions to their solution, and to ensure that solutions to problems are applied.

These categories will be used in analysing the various programmes of the DSIR. The individual pattern of sponsorship applies particularly to the successive allocation of awards to postgraduate and senior research workers in the universities (Chapter 7). The collective pattern is of special relevance to the Advisory Council's concern with the same central research establishments and co-operative research units over time (Chapters 4 and 5). Nevertheless, because of the importance of these organizations in financial terms and in representing the style of the department's administration, they go a long way toward setting the DSIR off from the other research councils. At the same time, this pattern draws attention to the fact that, from the Advisory Council's own point of view, the research stations and research associations were especially problematic. Through positions in their consulting and governing machinery, industrialists were able to suggest problems for research. The scope and direction of research was strongly influenced by the estimated needs of the 'traditional' sectors of industry. The question was, therefore, not only how to achieve a proper balance within the programmes of research but how to design research organizations in such a way that the views of manufacturers would be expressed. As will become apparent, the manner in which this question was answered was to have important consequences. Not the least of these was the failure of the Advisory Council to deal effectively with the challenge which was presented to it by independent developments in the organization of government science (Chapter 6). As a prelude to the main discussion and a source of illuminating contrasts with later developments the early history of the DSIR is treated in the following chapter.

2

The origins of the DSIR

The outbreak of war with Germany in August 1914 is an important event in the developments leading up to the inception of the DSIR.[1] With the commencement of hostilities a wide range of manufactured goods hitherto imported from Germany were found to be in short supply. These goods were of vital importance in the conduct of the war itself.[2] The shortages had occurred in fields of production which owed their development to discoveries in the physical sciences — more particularly in chemistry, the first science to be widely applied.

This crisis merely confirmed what perceptive observers had been saying for many years. Throughout the nineteenth century influential 'statesmen of science' had pointed out that there were few applied scientists working in British industry, and that many were poorly paid and were not used in ways which drew upon their scientific knowledge. Nevertheless, the events of 1914 served to create a sense of profound shock. They were a dramatic illustration of what could be achieved. By demonstrating conclusively the effectiveness of German scientific institutions, the industrial crisis reinforced the growing conviction that research undertaken as a large-scale, systematically organized activity could achieve definite results, and that the results were likely to have far-reaching utility in the realm of practical, everyday industrial affairs. But in addition to this, and of far greater significance, was the fact that unlike previous demonstrations of foreign achievement — the Paris Exhibition of 1867, for example — the wartime shortages presented Britain with a situation necessitating not only re-evaluation of her organization for science but the bringing about of certain desired changes if national disaster were to be averted.

The origins of the DSIR

British Dyes Limited

Rapid and effective action to mobilize existing scientific men and facilities for the purpose of carrying on the war could be undertaken only by the government. But because there was no administrative machinery for promoting and supporting scientific research, the task had to be taken over piecemeal by the established administrative departments. On the civil side, the most pressing and immediate problems were located in the industrial sphere and consequently fell to the Board of Trade rather than the Board of Education.

The shortage of dystuffs had placed the British textile trades in a grave situation. A committee appointed by the Board of Trade under Lord Haldane to consider the question was informed by a large and influential group of users of dyes that the textile industry would welcome public action. A subcommittee, which was subsequently formed under the chairmanship of Lord Moulton, came to the conclusion that the assistance of the State was necessary. On 22 December 1914 the Government announced a scheme for establishing a large dye manufacturing company. The company, to be known as 'British Dyes Limited', was to be floated with an advance of £1 500 000 payable in 25 years. An additional grant of £10 000 was provided over a period of ten years for the employment of large numbers of chemists, the provision of well-equipped laboratories, and the inclusion of technical experts in the directorate. An equivalent sum was to be raised from the contributions of interested firms.

While these proposals were being drawn up, and for some months after, the Government was under constant pressure from the scientific community itself. Criticism, comment, and advice were offered by eminent men of science both as individuals and as spokesmen for their societies and associations.

The British Science Guild, the Institute of Industry and Science, and the Royal Society

The scientists expressed concern at the neglect of science in Britain. In a letter to *The Times* of 18 August 1914 Sir William Tilden pointed to the existence of chemical knowledge, skill, and judgement, and urged that every effort be made to utilize them for the manufacture of synthetic dyestuffs. He did not suggest government action, but when such action was taken it was, on the whole, warmly supported and encouraged. Others who were more critical stressed the limited value of *ad hoc* emergency measures. Nevertheless, to the critics, as to the admirers of the Government's proposals for dyes, the future industrial development of the country depended on further, more far-reaching action.

One of the most influential of the organizations engaged in advancing the claims of science was the British Science Guild. The Guild, which had been founded by Sir Norman Lockyer in 1905 to establish a broader role for science in public life, took advantage of the opportunity created by the war to urge that public funds for the support of research be increased. It established its own journal in 1915, with the help and guidance of Richard Gregory, the assistant editor of *Nature,* who also helped to commit the older publication more firmly to the common task. In a series of crusading articles, Gregory severely impugned the existing level of public provision for science, and called for a complete reappraisal of its place in the national life.

Further weight was added to these demands by the Institute of Industry and Science, an association of scientists and industrialists established in 1915, which proposed a Ministry of Industry to develop essential industries and to deal with the related problems of research and education.

The Royal Society also played an important, though indirect, role in mobilizing scientific opinion. In an article in *Nature,* Sir William Ramsay drew attention to developments in France, pointing out that on 4 August 1914 the French Academy had appointed four committees to bring the views of scientists to the notice of the Government. His suggestion that the Royal Society should take similar action was accepted by the Council and on 5 November 1914 committees were appointed for chemistry, physics, and engineering to meet the Government's growing need for scientific assistance. However, being unwilling to sponsor any recommendations directly affecting the Government or industry, the Council of the Royal Society restricted its committees to questions of a purely scientific nature. As a result, they were unable to deal with some of the most important problems which came before them. Sir William Crookes, President of the Royal Society, and a number of Fellows of the Royal Society and the Chemical Society felt compelled to take independent action. Memoranda were addressed to the Government directing attention to the need for an effective policy with regard to the chemical industry and a deputation was formed to put the views of British chemists. The Government was asked to set up a standing national chemical advisory committee to provide information, to assist industrial research, and to help establish closer relations between research workers, teachers and manufacturers. J.G. Pease, President of the Board of Education, informed the chemists on 6 May 1915 that a scheme had been approved by which substantial additional assistance would be given by the Government to scientific education and industrial research. The Government, it turned out, had been working along lines which at least partly met the scientists' demands.

The problem of scientific manpower

The need for long-term action had first become apparent in March 1913 when a consultative committee under the chairmanship of A.H. Dyke Acland was appointed to inquire into the provision of university scholarships and exhibitions. However, the Board of Education was forced by the war with Germany, which brought the process of transmitting scientific knowledge and skills in the schools and universities almost to a standstill, to put aside its long-term plans for extending scientific education. Some preliminary findings of the Dyke Acland Committee, presented in December 1914, caused alarm. There were only an estimated 250 teachers and 400 full-time students in the universities of England and Wales, and in higher technical institutions only 50 such persons doing research with a bearing on industry. A small confidential committee was immediately formed under Sir William McCormick, chairman of the Advisory Committee on Grants to the universities, to consider the most suitable arrangements for developing teaching and research. The Committee expressed concern over the chaotic state of arrangements for holding examinations and awarding scholarships and recommended the institution of a national scheme of advanced instruction and research in science to 'promote increased uniformity within, and better articulation between, levels in the educational system.'[3] An important part of the scheme was concerned with enabling those who had already received higher instruction in science to undertake research. A central advisory committee composed of a small number of 'scientists, traders and other persons selected because of their personal fitness' was to allocate money from a central fund for this purpose. It was to these arrangements, outlined in a memorandum submitted to the Cabinet in the first week of May 1915, that the President of the Board of Education referred in his reply to the deputation from the Royal Society and the Chemical Society. Announcing the Government's plans in the House of Commons on 13 May 1915, the President of the Board of Education declared that it was his department's intention that the scheme should, when the present crisis had passed, form an integral part of its evolving plans for dealing with the place of science in the educational system as a whole. These intentions remained unfulfilled.

From the procurement of manpower to the organization of science in industry

In deciding to go ahead with the Pease plan, the Government resolved to create a body concerned with fostering the growth of applied science in industry. The Advisory Council, as the projected central advisory committee came to be called, was charged with the very general tasks of initiating proposals for: '(i) instituting specific researches; (ii) establishing or developing institutions or departments for the scientific study of problems affecting particular industries; (iii) the establishment and award of Research Studentships and Fellowships'.

The Government's decision attracted a certain amount of criticism from some Fellows of the Royal Society. This group, composed mainly of chemists, had looked forward to the Royal Society being invited to form the nucleus of the proposed national chemical advisory committee. They now formulated an alternative scheme for the nomination from among the Fellows of the Royal Society of a 'chemical council of state' to assist government departments in dealing with problems requiring scientific investigation. Sir William Ramsay, the leading spokesman, proposed that the Royal Society itself be formally constituted as a national scientific council with the duty of advising ministers of state. But the Council of the Society was unsuited for this, as critics of the proposal, which was not officially supported by the Royal Society, were quick to point out. Officials in the Board of Education decided to invite those government departments which made use of the findings of scientific inquiry and the universities to co-operate with the Advisory Council in evaluating research needs and opportunities. It was decided also to try placating the activist wing of the Royal Society. In the final draft of the Government's scheme, a 'regular procedure for inviting and collecting proposals' was to be established to enable the Advisory Council to 'act in intimate co-operation with the Royal Society and the existing scientific or professional societies and institutes.'[4]

The scheme, which was published on 23 July 1915 and issued as a White Paper by the new coalition Government, made provision for a Committee of Council 'responsible for the expenditure of any new moneys provided by Parliament for scientific and industrial research.'[5] The advantage of this arrangement was that it provided coverage of the United Kingdom as a whole. The Committee of Council was established by Order in Council on 28 July 1915. A small 'Advisory Council composed mainly of eminent scientists or men actually engaged in industries dependent on scientific research' met for the first time on 17 August 1915. Sir William McCormick was administrative chairman of the Advisory Council. The other members were Lord Rayleigh, Sir George Beilby, William Duddell, Richard Threlfall, and Professors J.A. McClelland, Bertram Hopkinson, and Raphael Meldola. The Advisory Council was to make recommendations for the expenditure of money from a sum (£25 000 at first, £40 000 in the following year) placed at the disposal of the Committee of Council for the initiation of the scheme, and both bodies were to operate under the aegis of the Board of Education.

The Advisory Council attempted to assess the nature and magnitude of the problems involved in encouraging the development of industrial research. It was aided in making this survey by the various government departments and professional bodies with which the scheme envisaged it should co-operate.

Inquiries were made into the number and distribution of staff and postgraduate students in institutions of higher education. Although the small numbers and the uncertainty as to their status made the development of a definite scheme difficult, it still seemed possible to make tentative experiments by way of aid to individuals. An invitation was therefore issued to vice-chancellors and deans of faculties with a view to eliciting applications from advanced students wishing to embark on research of importance to industry.

The Advisory Council was nevertheless permitted a broader interest in the range and direction of existing lines of research. Turning to research financed by organizations other than the universities and technical colleges it became convinced of the importance of awarding grants to prevent the termination of certain projects started before the war and supported from a number of sources. Specialized standing committees — for engineering, for metallurgy, and for mining — roughly half of whose members were to be nominated by the appropriate professional societies, were formed to deal with these matters. The movement in support of the extension of industrial research was found to be more widespread than had formerly been supposed. 'The practical man of business, the manufacturer and the trader', observed the Advisory Council, 'have been as anxious and interested as any.'[6]

The number and source of requests for funds suggested a certain amount of 'spontaneous' co-operation in the financing of research. Such arrangements had been initiated through the trade associations and professional institutions in response to the loss of foreign markets and the cutting-off of supplies of raw materials. For example, an application was received from the Glass Research Committee of the Institute of Chemistry under Professor Raphael Meldola. The work of this committee had been started by a number of the largest steel manufacturers, threatened in the earlier months of the war with the exhaustion of reserves of chemical glassware. With the Committee's encouragement Professor Herbert Jackson discovered a process for manufacturing a number of glasses necessary for the testing of materials and products. When the Institute reached the end of its funds, it submitted an application to the Advisory Council. Similarly, support was requested for investigations directed by Dr. Mellor, Principal of the Stoke Pottery School. They had been set in motion by the Staffordshire Pottery Manufacturers' Association in response to the difficulty in obtaining Seger cones, which were necessary as a guide to the firing of china and earthenware. The Advisory Council was asked for a special grant to establish laboratories and workshops at the Stoke School.

Demands of this kind gave rise to the conviction that the Advisory Council could more effectively fulfil the purposes for which it had been formed by extending its activities to include the provision of support to researches carried out in direct response to industrial needs. It was decided to take advantage of the opportunity offered by the wartime wave of co-operative action to build up a programme of publicly aided industrial research.

Research-minded trade associations were assured of the Advisory Council's willingness to consider applications for financial assistance. Other associations were exhorted to treat research as one of the common problems to which their funds should be devoted. One result was the sponsoring of investigations into the de-gumming of silk by the Silk Association conducted at Imperial College. Interest in prosecuting research with the encouragement of the Advisory Council was shown by employers' associations in the chemical, engineering, shale oil, and printing industries.

The opportunities for promoting research sponsored co-operatively through the trade associations proved to be limited. Many industries were without well-supported trade associations interested in organizing research into common problems. Others lacked strong professional societies. In the chemical and textile industries, for example, firms generally considered investment in research to be hazardous and unnecessary; in the rubber industry they did not participate actively in the association and their objectives were limited to the pursuit of common commercial interests. In industries such as glass manufacture there was a strong sense of the need for research and well-supported trade and technical associations. But these bodies were unsuited to the administration and conduct of research. For one thing, participation in them was voluntary and part-time. Since their administrative machinery for handling even the ordinary run of business was slight they were unable to assume responsibility for the supervision of continuous, large-scale research projects. Because they were primarily devoted to the pursuit of business and professional goals, there was the possibility that at some future date restrictive practices might develop. Research would also be likely to suffer by the exclusion of firms which, though willing to co-operate in research, were unprepared to become members.

The Advisory Council remained optimistic. Still, as an instrument for the organization of research the national network of trade associations was clearly inadequate. If, however, its expectations in this direction were unfulfilled it was more than ever concerned with the position and prospects of research in industry. Not only did it make further grants to the trade associations and professional societies, but it persisted in its idea of developing an industrial research programme by subsidizing investigations sponsored on a co-operative basis by industry. Meanwhile on 29 September 1916 the Board of Education's consultative committee issued its report on scholarships for higher education. It acknowledged the Advisory Council's developing role in this field, observing that responsibility for postgraduate training in research belongs to 'the Committee of the Privy Council . . . [and is] a matter for national organization and funds.'[7] The implied administrative division was endorsed by the Advisory Council. The new scholarship scheme, it commented, 'may be sufficient for academic purposes but not for . . . industry, commerce and agriculture.'[8] At the same time, it became increasingly apparent to several of the Advisory Council's members that the broadening of its sphere of operations to include the promotion of research carried out in industry made necessary a reconsideration of the Advisory Council's role in the Government. The provision of support on a greatly increased scale and the development of the complex system of central co-ordinating machinery required to administer it would be manifestly inappropriate under the Board of Education.

Replying to a deputation from the Board of Scientific Societies on 1 December 1916 urging increased support for scientific research, Lord Crewe, Lord President of the Privy Council, announced that responsibility for 'scientific and industrial' research — of which industrially-oriented postgraduate research was considered to be an integral part — was to be embodied in a fully-fledged administrative department. The government had also recognized, he said, the need for further financial assistance. In view of the unpredictable nature of likely expenditure on co-operative research in industry a lump sum of £1 million was to be entrusted to the Committee of Council* to cover operations during the next five years.

* The Lord President and the ministers who held places *ex officio* were designated by Royal Charter the 'Imperial Trust'.

The idea of the DSIR

On the assumption that it would be impossible to improvise a system at the moment when hostilities ceased, consideration was given in the closing months of 1916 to ensuring industrial support for applied research after the war. A comprehensive scheme was needed for securing more general acceptance of the co-operative principle. This was to be the responsibility of the Advisory Council, a small body composed of scientists and industrialists serving in their capacity as individuals.

The Advisory Council's terms of reference allowed for wide discretion. Proposals for research were to be referred to the Advisory Council; it was to initiate proposals, and, if requested, to give advice to the departments of education and other government departments.

The DSIR in the machinery of government

After the war, the machinery for watching over the execution of industrial science 'policy' was maintained and strengthened. An Order in Council of February 1929 terminated the original mixed ministerial and non-ministerial membership of the Privy Council committee, which assisted the Lord President in his duties. Both the Imperial Trust (corresponding changes in its membership were made by an Order in Council of April 1928) and the Privy Council committee came to consist of the Secretaries of State for the Home Department, for Dominion Affairs, for the Colonies (after 1947, Commonwealth Relations), for Scotland, the Chancellor of the Exchequer, and the Presidents of the Board of Trade and the Board of Education (after 1944, the Minister of Education).

The Advisory Council's task of assessing the potential fruitfulness of proposals submitted to it could be carried out only by people who by training and experience were capable of taking a comprehensive view of new scientific developments. A premium was therefore placed on scientists with intimate knowledge of the field in question and personal knowledge of the research workers concerned. Men were appointed who either had special knowledge of scientific issues likely to have a bearing on industrial problems, or direct experience of these problems coupled with an awareness of how they might be attacked through research. The scientists appointed to the Advisory Council were mostly senior men of established reputation; 89 per cent of all members for whom information is available held a first degree in a scientific or technological subject. A majority of the 107 were primarily engaged in university teaching and research.

Fifty-three per cent of the members were Fellows of the Royal Society. Of those actively engaged in scientific research, 22 were physicists, 23 chemists, and 18 engineers. Two were metallurgists, two mining engineers, and four botanists. Two were economists. Anatomy, astronomy, geology, mathematics, biochemistry, and zoology each accounted for one member of the Advisory Council. Other persons chosen for their scientific knowledge or administrative experience sat on the research boards and committees to which responsibility for the supervision of particular programmes was delegated.

The business of the DSIR, apart from the scientific and associated executive work carried out by the directors of research, was conducted by the administrative staff (their numbers rose from 11 in 1915 to 56 in 1963) under the secretary. The post was held by Sir Amherst Selby-Bigge (1915-16), Sir Frank Heath (1916-26), H.T. Tizard (1926-8), F.E. Smith (1928-46), E.V. Appleton (1947-9), Sir Ben Lockspeiser (1949-56), and Sir Harry Melville (1956-64).

The assumption by the Government of some responsibility for promoting scientific research of importance to industry in 1916 was perhaps long overdue. But in adopting these proposals the Government had done something more than this. The established departments of State were aware of and in some cases concerned with the problems with which it was proposed the DSIR should deal. They were interested in research in so far as it affected aspects of their broader administrative responsibilities. But their central concerns lay elsewhere. Consequently, insufficient attention was paid to increasing the output of trained research workers from the universities and to promoting research and development in industry. Where research was conducted into administrative and industrial problems, basic research tended to be neglected. Other researches were neglected because they were not closely related to any existing administrative field. At the same time, the results of research sometimes failed to find application because the departments concerned tended to ignore information which challenged the policy to which they were committed and for whose execution they were directly responsible.

Within the DSIR, research was to be more than a means to an end. It was to be an object of policy in its own right. For this reason, the recommendations of the Advisory Council would have to 'represent the progressive realization of a considered programme and policy'[1]

Statements explaining the DSIR to the 'outside world' made by Lord Haldane, Lord Balfour, Sir Frank Heath, and Henry Tizard in the early and middle inter-war period did much to underline this conception. The new Departement was to conduct research into large-scale problems affecting the welfare of the community as a whole, to promote research in industry and to stimulate the output of trained scientific and technological manpower.

The Advisory Council

The proposals of the architects of the DSIR carried novel administrative implications. If scientific research was to be supported and encouraged it would be necessary to give fuller administrative expression to the relatively new concept of government sponsorship of research.

However, the initial recommendations contained in the Pease memorandum of May 1915 were formulated not so much on this assumption, but rather in the belief that not only legislation but 'controversial issues' should be avoided. The Committee of Council for Scientific and Industrial Research and its Advisory Council were constituted by Order in Council, not by statute. The Central Advisory Council (the Advisory Council in the final scheme) was, moreover, to be 'as small as possible . . . [and] should not represent interests'.[2] 'By and large', wrote Sir Amherst Selby-Bigge, Secretary of the Board of Education, 'the [Advisory Council's] business will be to lick into shape and recommend proposals that come to them, rather than to sit down and devise original proposals.'[3]

It was not considered desirable 'to concentrate under the control or supervision of a single authority all the industrial research at present conducted by, and on behalf of, government departments.' Such an attempt, it was felt, might 'create friction and disturbance of existing interests'. It was, therefore, 'essential that the Advisory Council should work in close touch with Government departments concerned with research'. The principle regarding the size and composition of the Advisory Council, which was upheld at the time of the drafting of the scheme when it was suggested by the Treasury that the Royal Society should be invited to administer grants, was later reaffirmed in reply to a petition from the five great engineering societies requesting the appointment of additional members more particularly identified with important branches of industry. Its role as co-ordinator of research received less emphasis in later years when the Advisory Council as the centre of the newly formed DSIR was playing a more positive role in the organization of research. Indeed, at one stage a proposal was drafted for viewing the DSIR as 'the nucleus of what may become the national organ of intelligence and research'. Nonetheless, the original conception remained substantially unchanged. The task of providing information and advice seemed sufficiently straightforward for the Haldane Committee on the machinery of government to deal with, simply by the stipulation that those responsible for research should work 'in closest collaboration with the administrative departments concerned'.[4]

More significant than either of these themes was the discretion reserved to the Advisory Council in executing decisions. It was to adopt the role of an advance guard, going ahead in the van of scientific advance to identify and prepare the ground for the assault on major objectives. 'Effort' was, 'in the main, to be concentrated on lines desirable in the national interest, but which otherwise are unlikely to be pursued'. Once stimulated, research would be taken up by other bodies as they became interested in the work, leaving the DSIR free to withdraw and go on to something else. So attractive was this conception that within a few years of the DSIR's inception it became a model on the basis of which a new administrative approach was extended to other sectors of civil science policy. As far as research conducted outside an administrative department was concerned, the Haldane Committee stated, 'a form of organization on the lines already laid down for Scientific and Industrial Research will prove most suitable'.

Yet, as the Haldane Committee was forced to acknowledge, the idea of the DSIR 'had grown up in response to the pressure of a practical need and not in the pursuit of a reasoned policy'. When it was established it was not certain that the State could deal in any systematic and effective manner with research. Reflecting this aspect of its early development was the limitation of its function to the examination of proposals which came to it and the co-ordination of research carried on elsewhere. The exercise of initiative was to be confined to watching over scientific projects which were felt to be timely, but whose results would neither be assured nor foreseen.

The new arrangements would clearly have to be developed on the basis of experience gained in working out what was, very largely, an experiment. Nevertheless, to what extent was the Advisory Council to direct research in the light of national needs and to what extent was it to co-ordinate a group of independent research units? What dilemmas were to be involved in attempting to sustain these two roles and what were their consequences likely to be? The idea of the DSIR certainly facilitated the adaptation of the organization to the situation which confronted its early protagonists. But it also involved an unrealistic appraisal of the powers which were necessary if the somewhat ambitious place envisaged for it was to be achieved. While the idea helped to reconcile differing views about the organization of research it did not eliminate the fact of differing degrees of interest in research. At the same time, it raises the question of whether the tension between freedom and constraint, between planning and the 'free market' in research, might not only remain unresolved but be unresolvable.

4

Co-operative research

Under the government's 'Scheme for the Organization and Development of Scientific and Industrial Research', published in 1917, encouragement was offered to any group of firms associating for the purpose of sponsoring research into problems of common interest and undertaking to contribute to the cost. The grants were calculated on a general basis for a five-year period, the recipients undertaking to raise the sums required to justify them. The response from industry, although not great in the first few years of the scheme, was encouraging: 23 research associations were formed before 1924. This was not maintained. By 1923, co-operative research in a number of industries had collapsed. Between 1923 and 1925 more research associations were wound up than new ones formed. The research associations which failed were unable to attract the required level of support from their industries. Between 1928 and 1934, although the total income of the research associations remained unchanged, the industrial income of several research associations fell. The development of the research associations suggests that the judgement of the government in 1916 concerning the possibilities of organizing for research in industry in the post-war period was unsound. It was the circumstances of their inception after the war, not the conception of the programme during the war, that conditioned the development of the research associations.

The Advisory Council considered itself bound to safeguard the national interest where discoveries were made with the assistance of Parliamentary funds. A co-operative research association was expected to conduct research into problems of common interest to the industry and, where necessary, to communicate the results to other industries. The Advisory Council reserved the right of veto in the case of a proposal by a research association to sell any results of research to a foreign person or corporation. It further undertook to mediate in the event of a divergence of opinion between two or more research associations regarding a joint research and to act as arbitrator in the case of appeals arising from disputes as to whether a project was in the interests of the membership as a whole. The expectation underlying the programme was that support from public funds would not be needed in the long run. 'The larger and more prosperous industries', the Advisory Council said, 'might be expected . . . to find themselves both willing and able to continue the work of research without direct assistance from the state'.

The reaction to the Government's scheme

The DSIR was represented on the governing bodies of the research associations by two persons nominated by the Industrial Grants Committee. Inquiries concerning the possibility of appointing a non-voting assessor met with fairly general acceptance. A few research associations were wholeheartedly in favour. The replies of others revealed a certain evasiveness.

A small but important group of associations expressed reservations. The feeling of the Electrical and Allied Manufacturers' Research Association that discussions would perhaps not be so 'full and frank'[1] was echoed by the British Launderers' Research Association, which confessed to being 'somewhat uneasy about the proposal'.[2] 'The suggestion had', it pointed out, 'come at a time when the council felt that the Department's representatives . . . had had a good deal to say in directing the work of the Association and certain members . . . considered that it was time that representatives of the industry should exercise a little more voice in the management'. Nevertheless, the majority of research associations were not opposed to the idea in principle.

Perhaps the most pressing problem facing the Million Fund Committee* was the consideration of proposals for the formation of new research associations. It was necessary to explain the Government's scheme to the industries and to guide them in the drafting of preliminary plans. Large units of production, it was recognized, were not necessarily the ones most likely to come forward. 'No suggestion', it was observed, 'has ever been made . . . that the manufacturers of heavy chemicals or of iron and steel should establish Research Associations'. The scheme's appeal was also considered to be small in industries where economic units were small (e.g. pottery); in industries which employed a small amount of capital (e.g. needles, buttons, pins); and in industries which did not

---

* The Million Fund Committee was formed in 1923 to advise on expenditure of the fund of £1 million. It was succeeded by the Industrial Grants Committee in 1927.

depend on scientific knowledge (e.g. goldsmith's work, tailoring, millinery).[3]

There was opposition of a more articulate kind from bodies which were concerned with the organization of research in industry. The Labour Party and the Trades Union Congress considered the Government's plan ill-conceived and therefore unlikely to achieve success. Worse, by introducing what they described as a 'pernicious system' it had prejudiced the outcome of future schemes. In a document drafted in June 1924 the Government was accused of having failed to exercise effective control.[4] By 'control' was meant control over the choice of scientific staff, selection of directors on grounds of executive ability, and recognition that the supply of scientific manpower was too limited to support the rapid growth in the number of research associations.

To a vocal section of the National Union of Scientific workers (NUSW) the scheme of co-operative research was to be condemned for its failure to confer the benefits of research on the public in general and the Associations' employees, who were denied rights of ownership in discoveries and inventions. Professor Frederick Soddy, who was one of the scheme's most active opponents, believed that 'science — government science — is being step by step built up; not for humanity but its masters; not for the community, but big business'.[5] The State, he felt, should have reserved the right to veto researches which were judged to be contrary to the interests of the people. Instead, large sums of money were being handed over for the prosecution of research the results of which were the exclusive property of industry.[6] Other scientists, of whom Sir William Bragg was one of the most distinguished, were more moderate in their views, considering that scientists should prepare themselves for the position of greater equity and responsibility that would come to them as co-operative research gradually acquired a valued place in the life of industry. Furthermore, competition, by compelling individual firms to utilize the results of research conducted on a co-operative basis, was likely to ensure that any advantages to the consumer were passed on within a fairly short period. Indeed, the gains to the firm from membership of a research association required underlining. This the Government sought to do when it included a clause in the *Notes on the Articles of Association* protecting the firm against any proposed investigations which might seriously prejudice its market position. A firm which had established a predominant position in a certain field, but which under the constitution of the research association was obliged to submit to the wishes of the majority in matters of co-operative research, was to be allowed to appeal to the department.

Co-operative research

An important section of British industry appears to have acquiesced, if not shared, in the expectations of the scheme's protagonists. However, implementing it proved to be difficult. Many scientists and businessmen were outspokenly sceptical. Critics in the press often misunderstood or misrepresented it. Many firms were uncertain about associating for research and were hesitant, while others felt that the government's scheme was unnecessary as they were already doing research. A further group considered that other efforts by the government (of which the board of directors of British Dyes Ltd. was felt to be an example) had been unfairly exploited.[7]

Support without control

Negotiations with industries contemplating forming a research association were often carried on with committees of manufacturers formed to crystallize and promote local interest. The Department's officers were at pains to place their 'missionary efforts' in perspective. The financing of research on a quinquennial basis was to protect planned development from pressures of political expediency. The fact that subsidies were provided on the basis of formal, universally applicable terms of grant could be expected to discourage practices designed to influence the Industrial Grants Committee. The DSIR had further decided to abandon customary modes of administering support to research. Not only would the 'cost of administering small sums of money (which would be necessary if unexpended balances were to be returned at the end of the year) be excessive', but a 'harassing and unnecessary system of financial control would be built up'.[8] By agreement with the Board of Inland Revenue industrial contributions were to be recognized as business costs of the firm, and were not to be subject to income or excess profits taxes. In addition to associations formed to pursue research, the Department expressed its willingness to consider other bodies as eligible for financial assistance. Between 1915 and 1920 grants were given to 32 scientific and professional societies in aid of 62 researches at a cost of £68816.

Prompted by the desire to get a better picture of their accomplishments as a basis for deciding whether to extend grants for a further five-year period, the Advisory Council decided in 1922 to appoint 'visiting committees' composed of officers of the Board of Trade and the DSIR, at least two persons of high scientific standing, and in some cases a scientist with industrial experience not officially connected with the DSIR. In the following year the Advisory Council agreed that the Department should nominate two voting members of the research association councils. However, as it emphasized at an informal meeting with representatives of the Cotton Research Association in 1919, 'the powers of control reserved to the Department are only those necessary to secure co-ordination'.[9]

The councils and the directors of research

Membership of a research association was entirely voluntary: a firm could join or withdraw at any time. Any British firm was eligible and provision was made for the acceptance of full or associate members from other industries. The members were to have guaranteed rights of 'absolute ownership' and self-determination. Firmly-defined rights and obligations were to ensure the exercise of private initiative in these matters.

The research associations were given legal status under the Companies Act. A 'Committee or Board' was to select and prosecute research programmes, to hold research in trust for the benefit of members, and to determine the future scale of operations. It was to include 'as far as possible' representatives of capital, management, science, and skilled labour.

In addition to the DSIR representatives the 'Council', as it came to be generally known, in most cases comprised some twenty to thirty people from the industry[10] and up to six co-opted members (often including a trade union official). The council was answerable to the general meeting of member firms. At the general meeting firms elected members of the Council, a third of whom retired from office each year, and exercised their corporate responsibility for the running of the research association.

The directors of research were sometimes poorly equipped for the status of chief executive officer and head of the scientific staff. The first director of the Glass Research Association had no scientific qualifications, and in the Woollen and Worsted Research Association relations with staff were said to be spoiled by the directors's aloofness. Appointments in the photographic and non-ferrous metals research associations were also considered to be unfortunate. Other directors were very well qualified and a few, like Sir Herbert Jackson (scientific instruments), Dr. A.W. Crossley (cotton), and F.S. Sinnat (subsequently assistant director of fuel research in the DSIR) were of outstanding scientific abilities and attainments.

The research authorities were required to submit the programme of research for the coming year, which was drawn up by member firms represented on committees in conjunction with the executive staff, together with an estimate of expenditure, to the DSIR.

Co-operative research

Projects sponsored by a particular firm or group of firms and projected capital expenditure above a certain amount were subject to the approval of the Department.

Research associations whose members were related to each other as supplier and user or which had other aspects of their operations in common, a raw material for example, were expected to flourish. Firms could avoid duplicating research carried out in their own establishments, at the same time continuing to enjoy an advantage over non-affiliated competitors. Those in direct competition were expected to contribute because they could not afford to ignore a source of information likely to benefit others. Large incentives were nevertheless necessary.

The research associations in the industries

The earliest contracts were concluded on the understanding that in the case of income raised above a certain minimum sum the DSIR would contribute 'pound for pound'. Income above a second predetermined figure would be matched at a diminishing rate. Agreements concluded after 1923 and 1928 were based on a similar principle. The Advisory Council considered itself bound to resist political pressures for giving preferential treatment to firms who were members of research associations when awarding ordinary government contracts.

In the case of manufacturers who responded unfavourably to the issue of a non-voting representative DSIR officials found themselves unable to do anything. They were also forced to change some of their ideas concerning the research associations' mode of operation. Rather than establishing ties with universities and colleges in order to have their questions answered, they preferred to develop their own laboratories. Within an industry, firms were normally able to agree on priorities. Had outside help been widely requested it would undoubtedly have been complicated in some centres by pressure to assist several industries. Other, strictly financial, aspects of the scheme functioned to limit investment by firms. The research associations, for their part, were, in most cases, too little developed as working organizations to be able to offer a reasonable return in the form of scientific and technical services. Nevertheless, 2500 firms belonged to research associations by 1920.

In the Portland cement, woollen, electrical, printing, and non-ferrous metals industries, there existed bodies with a fund of experience derived from attempts to gather information, and sometimes to promote research on behalf of interested firms, which were of use to research associations or were incorporated by them. Others preferred, in their formative stages, to act as sponsors of research carried out in the laboratories of their 'learned society' or by members of the research association. The majority of research associations, including those which attracted a wide range of support, nevertheless found themselves in financial difficulties within a short time.

The research associations discharged their responsibilities toward the industries through the work of their scientific employees. Key qualifications were a degree in science or engineering, professional status, and publications. A non-graduate in his early thirties normally received about £200 whereas a young graduate with one or two years' experience and professional standing could expect a salary of about £400 per annum. About 250 persons of graduate or equivalent standing were employed by the research associations in 1930. The scientists became conscious of the overriding economic considerations behind co-operative research.

During the first major recession of the inter-war period (1922-5) intense competition for shrunken peace-time markets and the financial pressures of reconstructing capital equipment made research a poor investment for a large number of firms. The reorganization and, in many cases, liquidation of the 1931-4 period brought about a reduction in the subscriptions of many firms and forced others to withdraw from research associations altogether. The councils of the glass, shale oil, cutlery, silk, and motor and allied research associations, anxious to avoid losing the support of their members, felt compelled to accord primacy to *ad hoc* and immediately useful small investigations.[11] Longer-term work and more forward-looking projects often failed to get on the 'active' list.[12] The quality of much of the research undertaken, added to the conditions of financial insecurity, made the recruitment and retention of suitably qualified staff difficult.[13] Those that remained were sometimes hampered by an acute sense of personal insecurity (many were on short-term contracts lasting only three months in some cases) and by the absence of what a member of the board of British Westinghouse described as a 'corporate life'.

Of the research associations which capitalized on existing arrangements for promoting research, the Portland Cement Research Association became self-sufficient in 1923 and the Electrical and Allied Trades Research Association gained an early strength. However, two others, the Cotton Research Association and the Photographic Research Association, did equally well. The future of the other research associations depended on their capacity to stimulate an interest in research on the part of the smaller and least progressive firms.

Co-operative research

The research associations tried to increase their membership. Attempts were made to persuade businessmen of the value of co-operative research. Meetings attended by council members, directors of research, and research staff were held, petitions circulated, and addresses delivered to chambers of commerce.[14] Direct canvassing of firms was not uncommon and the cotton, electricity, non-ferrous metals, and refractories research associations employed liaison officers. The woollen, cotton, linen, and the boot and shoe research associations published popular handbooks and periodical bulletins summarizing published literature. In addition to the drain on the research associations' already meagre resources there was serious danger of the energies of their scientific staffs being deflected from their primary duty of research and development.

The relations with the industries and the extent to which the latter availed themselves in practice of the results of research were not the straightforward matter they were at first imagined to be. Smaller firms frequently had no one capable either of articulating research needs and putting them into scientifically meaningful terms or of understanding the concepts and terminology of technical literature and of relating these ideas to their own problems. Larger firms, however, particularly when faced with fierce price competition, either had limited reserves or preferred to devote the resources which were available to research within the establishment. Firms belonging to research associations were often reluctant to discuss their long-term projects with the research association staff for fear that information would be unwittingly passed on to other firms who were also members. In industries such as dyestuffs, where trade secrets were believed to exist, a powerful barrier existed against the formation of a research association. Moreover, co-operation did not occur even where it appeared possible in principle. User firms were unwilling to combine with makers where the latter held a monopoly. At the same time, large firms were somtimes in a position to run the research association in their favour. In some cases membership was of little importance to them. In others there were substantial differences of interest in research between the large firms and the smaller ones. In the Portland Cement Manufacturers' Association, for example, research was directed in a manner which suggested to outside firms that the benefits they were likely to secure were small. The same group of manufacturers had earlier expressed their preparedness to cut expenditure by half rather than associate with the 'least progressive' firms.

Trade support dwindled at an alarming rate in the cutlery, shale oil, and silk industries. Yet co-operative research in each had an auspicious beginning. The rubber and tyre, boot and shoe, and linen research associations, support for which had been confined to a very small proportion of firms, were marginally stronger. The majority of the research associations which continued some tradition of active organization for research failed to achieve financial independence.

At the end of the second quinquennium all the research associations faced uncertain futures. In 1923 it was clear that the minimum income which every research association was expected to raise was too low, and that the scale of operations of the majority was inadequate. Further government support appeared to be warranted. By 1928 the research associations, again in straitened circumstances, showed signs of alarm. A memorandum signed by the nineteen associations receiving grant-in-aid was placed before the Lord President of the Privy Council requesting continuation of the subsidy for ten years on a 'pound-for-pound' basis. Although grants were to be withheld from the glass, shale oil, cutlery, motor and allied, and motor cycle and cycle car research associations and from a number of professional and other bodies which the DSIR did not wish to strengthen, the Government decided to extend support for a further five-year period. Commenting on the decision *Nature* applauded its 'willingness to modify and adapt its policy to new facts and changed circumstances.'[15]

The end of the Million Fund

When the situation was again reviewed in 1933 the Industrial Grants Committee voiced its disappointment at the 'wholly inadequate bases on which the research associations with but few exceptions are working,' but declared themselves impressed by the considerable achievements of the research associations, which had resulted in large financial savings to their industries.[16]

The committee was prepared to urge 'a complete change of attitude by the Government'. 'If an industry will not find the money' (it said) 'the State must do so rather than let the associations disappear.'[17] Having considered the position the Advisory Council resolved on 14 February 1934 that '(i) in general increased support from public funds must be accompanied by increased support from industry; (ii) there were individual cases in which it might be necessary temporarily to give substantial grants at an early date in order to secure effective recognition of the value of research.'[18] The scheme of grants which was presented to the conference of the research associations expressed these concerns. A block grant guaranteed for five years in the first instance was offered. Above this, and up to a stated minimum, additional grants were to be made available to encourage expansion. Each case was to be assessed on its merits and grants were to be met from the Vote of the DSIR.

Between 1923 and 1928 subsidy payments fell from £103 000 to £54 000. In the period 1931-2 they fell from £80 000 to £66 000. The rise in the industrial subscriptions which began in 1931 was largely due to a broadening of the base of membership to include large consumers of the products of certain industries. It was too small to affect the general prospects of the movement.

By 1938 the subsidies paid to the research associations totalled £178 000. However, between 1933 and 1939 the contributions from industry rose from £167 000 to £372 000. Sixteen of the 18 research associations then in existence had experienced an increase of income of more than 50 per cent. The eventual withdrawal of Exchequer support was clearly no longer a realistic expectation.

In 1940 there were 21 grant-aided research associations with a total income of £480 000. Fifteen years later, in 1955, 39 research associations were in existence, in addition to eight research councils and other bodies in receipt of government grants. Twenty thousand firms representing over 50 per cent of British industry belonged to research associations. The number of persons on the staff who were of graduate status, mainly in science and technology, rose from 563 in 1944 to 1500 in 1956. The total income at the latter date was £4 700 000, of which the Government contribution was £1 300 000.

Attempts by certain sections of British industry between the wars to provide funds for the research associations by means of a compulsory levy collapsed. The limited success of these schemes expressed industry's unwillingness to commit itself to financing research in the absolute way that the DSIR in developing its grant policies had assumed to be attainable by the provision of generous inducements. Indeed, there is some irony in the fact that while the DSIR, in seeking to foster adoption of the compulsory principle, stressed the importance of numbers, industry chose to place the emphasis on the willingness of participants in the scheme.

The extension of industrial commitment on a voluntary basis in response to the competitive pressures which were present before 1939, but were enhanced by the experience of the war and the changed economic circumstances which flowed from it, accounts for such growth as the research associations underwent in the post-war period.[19] The favourable tax policy which was introduced in 1945 was a significant factor in the development of the research associations. Nevertheless, similar arrangements existed before 1939, and appear to have had only a marginal influence on the mobilization of support for industrial research.

If, after 1945, the continued existence of many of the research associations was no longer in doubt, and if the contributions of industry both grew in relation to expenditure by the DSIR and declined as a proportion of all industrial expenditure on research and development,[20] certain important problems remained which were no less intractable for being of a primarily administrative nature. Many research associations were without an adequate organizational basis for the performance of productive research. It became more and more difficult to co-ordinate the work of the research associations. Many firms were, moreover, marginal to several research associations, with the result that they were reluctant to join any one research association. Of greater importance in the latter half of the 1950s when the scheme once again entered a period of critical reassessment was the problem of stimulating research in key sectors of British industry, and simultaneously broadening the membership of the research associations to include firms in the traditional industries, which effectively resisted established techniques for mobilizing for research.

5

Corporate research

The centralization of government research facilities presented little threat to entrenched interests. The laboratories which grew up under the DSIR were *prima facie* likely to secure the appreciation of their services upon which they depended for success. The NPL, which had been administered since its foundation in 1899 by an executive committee appointed by the Royal Society with the aid of an annual Treasury grant, was taken over by the DSIR on 1 April 1918. In 1920 the Board of Education ceased to control the Geological Survey and Museum, which became the responsibility of the DSIR. A number of new laboratories were formed, sometimes in response to specific recommendations (e.g. forest products research, water pollution research) and sometimes in the expectation that those who were likely to benefit from research would be interested in the work (e.g. chemical research).

Considerable importance was attached to the provision of representation for interested bodies and professional and trade associations were encouraged to co-operate actively in the work of the central establishments. Nevertheless, the proposals for their creation must be read as statements of the potential contribution of research and development to certain important functions of government. As F.G. Ogilvie, Secretary of the Geological Survey remarked in a letter to Lord Curzon, 'there appears to be every ground for regarding the . . . transference of the Geological Survey and Museum as a step towards a logical amalgamation of State services.'[1]

The remuneration of scientists

The NPL was initially organized in two divisions, for physics and engineering. Five new divisions — metallurgy (1906), research into ships (1908), aerodynamics (1917), electricity (1918), and metrology (1918) — were formed by 1918, and the scope of its activities was broadened to cover fundamental physical and engineering research. When the DSIR assumed responsibility for the laboratory it not only inherited a vast body of expertise and the managerial assets of a going concern but it also acquired an institution of considerable intellectual force. After 1918 the Laboratory took on more work for industry and continued to do pioneering research in fields of importance to a large section of British industry. As the work developed in range and quality new divisions were formed (e.g. in 1940 the light division split off from physics).

The pre-eminence of the NPL within the DSIR's system of central research organization led to the Laboratory becoming the parent of new institutions. Highly developed divisions were taken out of the NPL (e.g. in 1954 the engineering division became the basis of a new Mechanical Engineering Laboratory). Existing research groups formed the basis of other laboratories. Research workers attached to government establishments or universities often worked independently for several years — the work of the Water Pollution Research Board between 1927 and 1939 is a case in point — before reorganization at a single centre.[2] The Government's estimation of applied science in relation to industry was expressed in an unenlightened policy towards the management of scientists and in the application of controls to scientific research. Heads of scientific organizations were expected to conform to certain requirements regarding appointments and other staff matters and they were obliged to work within a financial framework which was more appropriate to ordinary administrative expenditure.

In 1917, the Advisory Council stated that one of its principal aims was to raise the level of remuneration of scientists. The settlement which was reached was, however, unfavourable to scientists and engineers. Members of the higher echelons of the DSIR were responsible for appointing and promoting scientists in the early years. The scientists' position was shaped by the administrators' attitudes and by those of Sir Frank Heath, Secretary of the DSIR from 1917 to 1927. Heath's influence is difficult to estimate. What is certain is that he was a non-scientist, and on a number of occasions showed little understanding of scientists. Unlike his predecessor, Henry Tizard was sympathetic to their claims. That his achievements on their behalf were limited was due less to complacency than to the difficulty, once a general scheme of salaries was in force, of raising the level of reward in the Civil Service.

Corporate research

The scheme of salaries determined for the NPL was used as the basis for salaries in establishments other than the Geological Survey and Museum, which was without any firm arrangement until 1922. The Fuel Research Station, established in 1919, was only partly graded at first. The grading of the Chemical Research Station, formed in 1925, took more than a year. These staffs and the scientists working under the Food Investigation Board, the Building Research Board, and the Forest Products Research Board were treated as temporary employees. The NPL establishment was finally settled on 3 July 1925. (Grades and basic salaries ranged from principal assistant, £650 × £25 to £750, to junior assistant, £175 × £15 to £235.)

The salaries of the scientific grades were lower than those of the administrative branch.[3] Scientists received lower pay than administrators of similar age, qualifications, and experience. The discrepancy was particularly marked in the junior grades. A man entering the service as a scientific assistant in 1933 could expect a salary of £150. In the corresponding administrative grade — that of assistant principal — the same sum was available as an allowance in addition to the basic salary. Even allowing for the fact that the assistant principals were sometimes senior by a few years, the salaries were considerably higher — as much as £600 at the top of the scale. All the scientists had university degrees or equivalent qualifications.

The difference of treatment was not confined to the lower ranks. The estimation by the secretary and his advisers of the principal candidates for the posts of director of food research and superintendent of the Low Temperature Research Station at Cambridge provides a case in point. After the death of Sir William Hardy in 1934, Eric Barnard was appointed to the directorship at a salary of £1146. Barnard, who graduated from Oxford University with a second-class honours degree in physiology, had joined the administrative branch in 1919 as an assistant principal, where he rose to the grade of principal in 1923. As director he became responsible for all the scientific work at the Cambridge Station and the Torry and Ditton research establishments. The post of superintendent was given to Dr. Franklin Kidd. After carrying out important botanical research at Imperial College for which he was later awarded a D.Sc., Kidd was appointed principal assistant at the Low Temperature Research Station. In a letter to F.E. Smith in support of his candidature he wrote: 'Personally, I am convinced that the Board's reputation and future depend upon placing the principal emphasis . . . upon fundamental inquiry.'[4] Dr. Kidd was appointed at a salary of £939.

Scientists' careers

Between 1916 and 1925 a considerable number of scientific and technical staff were receiving what J.G. Wheeldon, establishment officer in the DSIR, described as 'practically personal salaries.' 'Each case that comes up for review and each new appointment', he pointed out, 'presents difficulties. Also we are not finding it too easy to attract suitable candidates because of an absence of any scale of pay or indication of prospects'.[5] The scientists employed by the Forest Products Research Board continued in their temporary status after 1925. The grounds given for the decision were that the Board's work was insufficiently advanced.

Opportunities for advancement for scientists within the government service were often limited. Commenting on the revised scale of salaries introduced in 1922, the staff association of the Geological Survey and Museum observed:

The number of Senior Geologists is expressly limited to 12. This means that an officer joining the staff at £300 inclusive reaches his maximum of £450 after 12 years of service. He may then have to wait an indefinite period for a vacancy in the grade of Senior Geologist before he proceeds to the maximum of £650.[6]

Senior scientists in other establishments often occupied quite 'junior' positions. One man of 46, with considerable experience, was appointed on an ungraded basis at a salary of £500.

The Advisory Council noted 'a certain class consciousness' among the younger men. The geologists, for example, compared their position with that of the administrative staff and declared that 'reorganisation of the staff here and . . . at HQ should have been carried out *pari passu.*' Establishment matters of concern to scientists were usually brought to the attention of the Institution of Professional Civil Servants. More commonly, dissatisfied scientists left the government service for higher-paid posts in industry, although the number of such posts was limited. In 1918 attention was drawn to an employee of the NPL receiving a salary of £200 who took a post at £450 in industry and to another who shortly after· being offered £300 accepted a job with a firm at £800. Of the newer establishments, the Building Research Station had a particularly high rate of resignations.

Commenting on the situation at the NPL, Sir Richard Glazebrook, the director, observed that while it was 'impossible to compete with commercial offers in the case of men who are out to make money', the scientists with whom he had to deal 'do not constitute such a class'.[7] But the conditions of service of the Government's scientific employees were not fully conducive to the conduct of research. Attendance at scientific meetings was not regarded as one of their duties, and leave was often grudgingly given. It was difficult, too, for the young scientist to move in order to work in the closest contact with those who were making promising advances in his field of research.

In the matter of consideration for promotion, administrative criteria loomed large. Administrative skills were considered important in the assessment of scientists' performance. Of the scientific officers at the Building Research Station to whom the Treasury agreed to make pay awards in 1925, for example, one was in charge of the records section and the other acted as deputy to the director both in dealing with outside people and in the general supervision of the work of the station. The taking on of additional duties thus became the basis for the provision of higher salaries. If a scientist was to improve his economic position he was obliged to assume more responsibility, often to the detriment of his professional concerns. Advancement therefore had drawbacks. Reginald Stradling said that on his appointment to the directorship of building research he had 'no time at all for research and very little for the direction of fundamental work'.[8]

The directors of research: financial procedures and administrative constraints

The place of the DSIR's laboratories within the central government determined the demands which were made upon the directors and their scientific staffs by the administrative staff of the H.Q. office. For example, one of the points stressed during the negotiations over the future of the NPL was that 'the arrangements for future finance will be those usual in government departments'.[9] The approved estimates were divided up under headings for the main branches of work. Expenditure under each heading was not to exceed the stated limit without the agreement of the secretary. Greater financial and administrative flexibility was considered necessary by the directors of research. However, proposals for a looser form of accounting at the beginning of the financial year, and, as an alternative, a system of supplementary estimates were rejected by the Government.

The disadvantages of annual accounting were manifest. The inflexibility was enhanced by the requirements of large-scale research. For one thing, there was no automatic relation between the allocation of funds for the purchase of an expensive piece of equipment and the acquisition of the staff necessary to run it. Because of this, and because of the large numbers of research workers and associated administrative organization and services, estimates had to be prepared earlier, with the result that they were often less reliable. With the growth in the capital requirements of research, there was an increase in the length of time between ordering and the delivery of a piece of equipment. The annual financial provision had to be used to pay not only for new orders but also for back orders maturing in that year, often at the cost of restricting the development of current programmes of research.

As regards staffing, no appointment was to be made for which Treasury approval had not been obtained. Changes in the numbers of staff within the various classes and grades required Treasury authorization. Glazebrook argued forcefully that a system of special increments was necessary, within a scheme of annual increments. There was, he pointed out, the man of exceptional gifts, whom it might be difficult to retain and who would merit special reward.

Then there is another case. The work is very various. Let us suppose a man high up in the Assistant Grade leaves; it is probable that in a Government Office someone just below this can take on his work and responsibilities, and will normally in a year or so receive the salary of the man who has gone. In the laboratory that is not so: the Assistant Class contains Physicists — and now these are much sub-divided into specialists in Heat, Optics, Acoustics, etc. — Engineers, Electricians, Chemists, Metallurgists, Naval Architects, Aeronautics experts etc. It may well happen that the only man who can replace A is a junior, M or N, not B or C — next in rank to A ... It would seem to me to be absurd to take a man from outside and put him in the vacant post and not be able to promote one of your own staff.[10]

Although discretionary appointments were eventually allowed by the Treasury in the case of scientific officers below the principal assistant grade, the general difficulty persisted. Permission was refused Glazebrook's successor, J.E. Petavel, to promote to higher grades a number of scientists in the assistant grades within the authorized limits on the grounds that 'further adjustment cannot be contemplated for some considerable time'[11].

As late as 1930 difficulties were being experienced in recruiting suitably qualified people, particularly to the junior grades at the NPL. Because the main task of the DSIR was seen as encouraging industry to employ larger numbers of scientists and to utilize them more effectively, it could not itself offer higher salaries to research workers but was compelled to base the scale of remuneration on the market price for this category of manpower. The Fuel Research Station, for example, attempted to restrict the range of salaries as closely as possible to market rates. The scale was apparently an underestimate. It was found to be 'impossible to attract persons of the necessary training and experience at the . . . salaries . . . proposed.'[12]

If the leadership of the DSIR was unable to attempt directly to enhance the financial attractiveness of the scientific career it could ensure that posts in the government service were open to the talented. This it failed to do. The legal rules governing Civil Service appointments precluded the appointment of non-British subjects. The effect of this, as Heath remarked, was that the 'whole American supply is cut off'.[13] The arrangement at the NPL whereby the scale applied to women as to men was regarded as 'abnormal'[14] and not extended to other establishments.

Increases in the salaries attached to positions occupied by scientists were affected by administrative considerations. In 1929 Tizard wrote to Balfour expressing his fear that 'on the present scale (of salaries) we shall not be able to attain or retain the services of good enough men'.[15] Significantly, however, he justified the difference between the proposed increase in the director of fuel research's salary and that of the director of food investigation on the grounds that the former laboratory was smaller and without direct association with industry. He added that this in no way reflected on the 'scientific distinction of the present holder'.[16]

The pattern of research in the newer establishments

The divisions of the NPL which were expanded and constituted independent laboratories often established themselves within a short period of time as national centres of research. However, there is some evidence that the separation of hydraulics and mechanical engineering research from the parent institution was premature. The Fuel Research Station, which originated independently of the NPL, similarly failed to live up to its early promise.

The central establishments played an important role in carrying out research of interest to industry as a whole and in solving problems which were wider than those of any single trade. Firms engaged in the supply of raw materials and a large proportion of firms in manufacturing industry were in many cases unable to formulate requirements for research and were lacking arrangements with which to apply the results of research performed in government laboratories. In some instances, secondary factors were most in evidence. One such factor — as in the case of forest products research after the dissolution of the Empire Marketing Board in 1933 — was the folding-up or decline of organizations which had previously functioned as foci of interest in research and as organs for its expression. In others, such as general engineering, the uncertainties associated with investment in research lay more or less directly behind the inability of management to show an awareness of the products and potential achievements of science. The initiation of research by the central establishments of the DSIR was accompanied by the continuing inability of the smaller firm in the longer-established industries to take charge of any aspect of projects prior to their having reached the final development stage. In addition, they were oblivious to the promise of research.

The research boards were concerned with the general problem of striking a balance between advisory and *ad hoc* work and longer-range research. The latter was usually performed at less than its cost to demonstrate the possibilities of research. As G.B.B.M. (now Sir Gordon) Sutherland, Director of the NPL from 1957 to 1964, observed:

A superintendent will say, 'I want to take this a stage further and build something because industry will not do it'. I wonder if this is correct. The more we spoon-feed industry, the less they will do for themselves. On the other hand, we must encourage industry. We must see that the thing is done one way or the other.

The consolidation of a strong research organization was often not achieved before a heavy burden of work for industrial organizations was taken on. Although limited as a proportion of total staff costs, standards work soon became the second largest division at the NPL. Measurement, analysis, and the testing of instruments tended to grow faster than other aspects of the laboratory's work. All the establishments received an increasing number of requests for special investigations and for advice on industrial problems. The Hydraulics Research Station, in particular, sought to provide fee-paid services, nearly a half of the running costs being recovered in this way. Other laboratories failed to gain the organized support of the profession. Leading practitioners were not always willing to sit on the Chemical Research Board and the Royal Institute of British Architects was described as 'critical, even hostile toward the Building Research Board'.[17] These difficulties were compounded by the absence in some fields of a well-developed body of theoretical knowledge. Without a strong tradition of fundamental inquiry the newer laboratories found difficulty in sustaining a policy of devoting a proportion of available resources to research which was only loosely related to the development of new techniques or the introduction of a piece of equipment. Directors of promise in the formative years of the central laboratories sometimes achieved solid but disappointing results. Certainly, strength of personality as well as energy and a sense of commitment was a necessary ingredient in building the prestige of an institution.

The NPL was not subject to these pressures to quite the same degree. It is true that the regulations regarding expenditure, promotion and appointments applied with equal force to all the establishments. However, owing to the circumstances of the DSIR

41

takeover in 1918,[18] the executive committee of the Royal Society stayed in being, and in the time which elapsed before his retirement in 1919, the director, Glazebrook, was able to establish a certain amount of autonomy in managerial matters. Practices current in the DSIR, mainly with regard to salaries, were not applied in the laboratory, and it was free in important respects from the discipline of a government department. At the same time, the association with the executive committee of the Royal Society, from whose guidance it benefited, conferred prestige on the NPL in the eyes of the scientific and scholarly world as well as the world of industry. Unlike the building and chemical laboratories, it did not serve a single 'disorganized' industry. Unlike the mechanical engineering and hydraulics research laboratories, the NPL was composed of a number of divisions each devoted to a distinct discipline or sub-discipline. The fact that it was thus diversified meant that the decline in vitality to which all fields are periodically subject could be absorbed: unexciting research could be contained where there were other subjects in which research was progressing. The size of the NPL (in the 1960s there were about 100 projects in progress at any one time and roughly twice that number of minor ones), the high morale of its staff and its relatively harmonious and stimulating relations with outside bodies contributed to its success. Its contribution to fundamental research in the basic physical and engineering disciplines permitted the laboratory to maintain its position as the scientific 'centre' of the DSIR.

In its capacity as prosecutor of research the Government was obliged to administer the funds which were made available for the conduct of research and to develop a policy for managing the group of scientists who were employed in the government service in growing numbers. In doing so, the Government overlooked what scientists considered to be the needs of research. They exacerbated a situation in which the importance of research was seldom acknowledged in political circles. It was not that the expert knowledge and skills of the scientists were denied or disparaged. Indeed, they were an established fact and the dependence of ministers and civil servants upon their advice in many technical matters was freely acknowledged. Rather, it was believed that the scientist, as well as the civil servant whose business is administration, could only function effectively *as a scientist* where his sphere of competence was clearly defined in relation to that of the administrator. Considered in this light, the subordinate position of the scientist was primarily a logical, not a social matter. The contribution expected of him rested on a principal of divided functions in which scientific work was sometimes of great importance in decisions, but scientists were of less weight as members of the bureaucracy. In seeking to maintain the distinction, however, rules and procedures were developed and applied by the class of administrators which threatened to render ineffective the heads of the various laboaratories, who in discharging their *executive* duties with regard to the programme of research had to elicit the best work from the scientific staff.

The neglect of policy implicit in the separation of administrative responsibility from responsibility to science was sustained by the system of annual budgeting. Directors were encouraged by the arrangement to apply unspent funds vigorously, with the result that a flurry of purchasing activity usually took place at the end of the financial year. For their part, the Headquarters staff considered it to be too difficult to frame general criteria for evaluating particular projects outside the terms of the annual agreements regarding expenditure and staff numbers. A system of frequent review with an eye to terminating unproductive research was not part of administrative practice. The way was therefore open for the continuation of research which had ceased to be closely related to national priorities in a given field.

6

The organization of government science

One of the first problems facing the DSIR following its inception in 1916 was that of co-ordinating its activities with those of other government bodies. Arrangements were made for relating its interests to those of other departments. The heads of the scientific organizations co-operated with each other. In the case of the MRC, and later the ARC, quarterly meetings were arranged between the three secretaries. Conferences attended by the biological secretary of the Royal Society were organized for the MRC, the DSIR, and the Development Commission. Otherwise, research programmes were drawn up in common form and discussed in annual meetings of the directors of all the establishments under the chairmanship of the DSIR's secretary. Assessors nominated by other departments took part in the discussions of the research boards and committees but were not entitled to vote.

The period following the First World War saw the initiation of much meteorological, agricultural, medical, and other research. The war itself had seen a growth in interest in research on the part of the service departments: the War Office, the Admiralty, the Ministry of Munitions, and the Air Ministry. The suggestion arose that the work of the various naval, military, and aeronautical research establishments might have civil applications. Of equal, if not greater weight, was the desire for economy in public spending on scientific research. An attempt was made to devise means to avoid overlapping both with each other and with the research organizations of the civil departments of state.

A Radio Research Board, formed on the recommendation of the Imperial Communication Committee of the Cabinet, was already in existence. The Cabinet Committee on the Co-ordination of Scientific Research under the chairmanship of Lord Balfour recommended that 'in relation to fields of scientific research which are of interest to the fighting services, boards be established on the lines of the Radio Research Board'[1] The Cabinet accepted the recommendation on 11 February 1920 and agreed to establish co-ordinating boards for physics, chemistry, and engineering. A Fabrics Co-ordinating Committee was formed later. The co-ordinating boards were '(i) to provide for the interchange of information between the various government technical establishments . . . (ii) to arrange for the communication of . . . information to interested parties outside the government service; (iii) in the case of researches not otherwise adequately provided for, to make the necessary arrangements to meet the requirements of Government departments and others'.[2] The DSIR was to be 'responsible for the provision of funds for research . . . [and] for securing contributions from industry and for co-operation with research associations where appropriate'.[3]

H.T. Tizard, Assistant Secretary of the DSIR, was placed in charge of the co-ordinating boards and given the title of Principal Secretary. They comprised a chairman who was a senior member of the Advisory Council, two members nominated by the DSIR of whom one was from the NPL, representatives from the service departments and independent scientists. Each board was placed under a Special Secretary.

The co-ordinating boards not only attempted to watch over the heterogeneous scientific work and to co-ordinate the different research groups of the services, but they also undertook research into a wide range of problems, including the silencing of aircraft, metal fatigue, the detection of X-rays, and the determination of the height of the Heaviside layer. An attempt was made to continue research which was in danger of being abandoned through lack of funds and to start exploratory work of potential interest to the services. Research which was largely, but not exclusively of civilian interest was also carried on the co-ordinating boards' grant. The Physics Board, for example, encouraged the extension of acoustical researches started by the Admiralty and the War Office for mainly civilian purposes. This and other research was performed at the NPL, and, to a lesser extent, at other DSIR research stations and the universities. But it was mainly carried out at the research stations of the armed services: the Royal Aircraft Establishment at Farnborough, the Woolwich Arsenal Experimental Station, the Admiralty Engineering Laboratory, the Admiralty Mining School, and the Signals Experimental Establishment.

Despite their accomplishments the co-ordinating boards proved unsuited to the task of surveying the growing number of active centres of investigation in the widening field of research related to both the improvement of industrial technology and the development of weapons.

A less formal system of co-ordination

Certain ambiguities appear to have been present from the co-ordinating boards' inception. As early as 1920 the Advisory Council noted difficulties in keeping in touch with the constantly changing points at which progress was being made in research. According to his biographer, Ronald Clark, Tizard himself soon became 'sceptical of what they might accomplish'.[4] In most cases it was necessary 'to make sure that decisions of the board for undertaking the special piece of work could be safely acted upon'. But that meant in effect satisfying itself that 'a decision would not be opposed by any of the Departments'. Similarly, in the case of 'research for the fighting services by private firms . . . the actual arrangements [were] not easy';[5] at that time the general relations of the DSIR with industry were not marked by mutual confidence. The boards had 'no executive control over Government establishments for research or equipment . . . '[6] Their authority extended only to technical matters: it was not supposed to be administrative. Yet co-ordination was often impossible 'without interference in the administrative functions of the services'. Much of this business was classified as confidential by the service departments. Thus 'any request for reports on all chemical researches' would, it was felt, 'only result in . . . [their] . . . withholding rather more in the future than they have in the past'.[7] Contrary to the expectations of the Secretary of the DSIR, the service departments do not appear to have been compelled by the threat of further cuts in their already depleted peace-time resources to consult the boards. Furthermore, the co-ordinating boards were unable to gain wholehearted acceptance of the idea of pooling information about research and its results under conditions of continuing inter-service rivalry. *Rapport* was therefore not easily established, and when established tended to be precarious and short-lived.

Attempts were made to formulate principles which would aid co-ordination. A combined meeting of the boards on 17 May 1922 established a more uniform policy. These procedures proved ineffective. Only that information the communication of which the service departments regarded advantageous was communicated. Much of what passed through the hands of the co-ordinating boards was incomplete or out of date. Early in 1927 a subcommittee of the Committee of Civil Research, appointed in response to a Cabinet inquiry of 18 October 1926 concerning economy in research, drew attention to certain major defects in the system of interdepartmental communication. The chief recommendation, which stated that the co-ordinating boards were not the best means of preventing overlapping and duplication of effort, was accepted by the Government. The Advisory Council urged that 'in accordance with the proposals (i) the co-ordinating boards for Chemistry, Engineering and Physics be dissolved: and (ii) the Radio Research Board be relieved of its co-ordinating functions'.[8]

On the advice of the subcommittee on the co-ordination of research, machinery was established for research having potential military applications similar to that which existed to co-ordinate the work of the DSIR and the civil departments, the Development Commission, and the MRC. The researches currently being supervised were divided between the DSIR and the service departments. As new activities requiring co-ordination grew up, new committees were formed: either new research boards with provision for external assessors, or, in the case of programmes in which two or more agencies actively participated, joint committees. Their efforts were reinforced by the development of numerous contacts among working scientists. Although the co-ordinating boards failed to develop a co-ordinating policy at a high level, their purely consultative role probably made it easier to foster an awareness among senior members of government scientific staffs of the aims and activities of their colleagues in other departments and so helped to prepare the ground for the more flexible liaison network which replaced them. By the latter half of the 1950s these arrangements were beginning to prove inadequate.

Government and scientific research

At the same time that the DSIR's central establishments and research associations were being developed important changes were taking place in the internal organization of government departments as they sought to come to terms with the same problems. A set of competing, and sometimes complementary, activities grew up, as a result of which the DSIR came to adopt a changed position within the overall organization of government science.

In the years following the demise of the co-ordinating boards the interest of government departments in scientific research was limited. Spending on research for civilian purposes reached approximately £4 millions by 1939. After 1945 resources were devoted by administrative departments in growing amounts to the maintenance of laboratories for the prosecution of research designed to solve problems relevant to the discharge of their executive functions and to promote technical advance in industry.

The National Research Development Corporation (NRDC) was established in 1948 to foster the development of inventions which would not otherwise attract a financial backing from private sources.

Within government departments a chief scientist's division or its equivalent was usually formed. These divisions often grew out of units with routine technical functions like the Ministry of Fuel and Power's Fuel Efficiency Branch, which was formerly responsible for increasing the efficiency of industrial and non-industrial plant. They were modelled on the wartime operational units attached to the service ministries and commands. Scientists employed in the 'scientific branch' were concerned with the solution of problems relevant to the practical requirements of administration. Increasingly, however, their energies were directed to enlarging scientific knowledge of the subject-matter of the various administrative departments. At the same time, a growing proportion of qualified scientists and technologists in the government service occupied positions at a sufficiently authoritative level in the formulation of policy to ensure effective technical direction of the work.

Expenditure on research underwent considerable expansion after 1945 and several departments undertook research virtually for the first time. The main departments were the Post Office (which was spending £5 millions a year on research in 1964), the Agriculture and Fisheries departments (£4 600 000), the Health Department, the Ministries of Power and Transport, the Home departments, and the Ministry of Public Buildings and Works (£3 million). The Ministry of Aviation, although concerned primarily with defence research, also undertook a considerable programme of civil research costing, in 1964, £25 millions. Two service departments, the Admiralty and the Air Ministry, were concerned with certain aspects of civil scientific research and spent almost £2 millions a year.

Corresponding to the increase in expenditure was the creation of laboratories and the expansion of existing ones. Large sums were devoted to full-scale experiments and field-work by the Ministry of Works; a Mining Research Station for the conduct of research into safety in coal mines and for the testing of equipment employed underground (and used for a number of years by the Factory Department of the Ministry of Labour) grew up under the Ministry of Power; the station at Dollis Hill conducted extensive researches on communication for the GPO (employing, in 1961, 240 research officers or about one-third as many as the DSIR).

The institutional arrangements for the conduct of research

provided the background for the emergence of new forms and new fields of organized research. In 1958, the Government announced a programme of space research, of which an important part — rockets and satellites — was placed in the hands of the Ministry of Aviation (formerly the Ministry of Supply). Space research — in which the DSIR was involved through researches in telemetry and data-processing — depends on knowledge from a range of disciplines. Moreover, it can be undertaken only with equipment which is itself the product of new and advanced technologies. By 1957 the rising costs of research in subatomic physics was creating problems of organization. The solution adopted was to establish a National Institute for Research in Nuclear Science financed through the Atomic Energy Vote by means of a grant to provide co-operative facilities for universities and other institutions for research in nuclear physics. A new centre of administration was thus added to a field which was already absorbing the largest single share of government funds available for civil research.

By the opening years of the post-war period, it was apparent that the assumption by the executive departments of a more positive role in the organization and direction of research was undermining the pre-war relationship between the government user and the 'researching' department. The House of Commons Select Committee on Estimates considered 'the line of demarcation . . . [to be] . . . not always clear'.[9] This appeared to be the case in building research (DSIR and the Ministry of Works), fuel research (DSIR and the Ministry of Fuel and Power), and fisheries and forestry research (DSIR and the Ministry of Agriculture and Fisheries and the Forestry Commission). Nevertheless, it was felt to be 'too early to decide what the ideal government organization for research should be'. The Advisory Council on Scientific Policy (ACSP), in particular,. was content to interpret the 'Haldane principle' more flexibly. In its first report, it recommended that:

(i) the executive department should be responsible for identifying problems requiring research, settling their order of priority, deciding where the various investigations should be carried out and applying their results.

(ii) the Research Councils, and particularly the various branches of the DSIR, should, as in the past, be free to initiate background research where they think fit . . . They should also undertake research at the request of the executive departments.[10]

In practice, reliance was placed on developing a 'first class system of liaison at all levels and the freest interchange of information not only on results but on projects'.[11] It is doubtful whether this aim was ever entirely achieved. For example, tenders received by the Ministry of Transport and Civil Aviation in 1956 for work to be done to new specifications were often not shown to the Road Research Laboratory, which also tended to be uninformed about how construction in accordance with new specifications performed in practice. But despite the deficiencies, the question of whether, where an ordinary administrative department as well as the DSIR was interested in research, the former should be asked to assume full responsibility, was never fully raised. Nevertheless, important changes were taking place the consequences of which became apparent in the closing years of the decade.

A problem of overlapping: the CSIR takes stock

The changes, which were so significant in the latter part of the 1950s, involved the assumption by government departments of a changed role in relation to the DSIR. They were not only beginning to conduct research; they were, on the basis of this, developing closer ties with industry, the public corporations, and a host of voluntary and other organizations. They thus found themselves the centre of co-ordination of research, both public and private, which was related to activities and operations for which they were formerly responsible only in a strictly administrative sense. A shift of this kind occurred in the national organization of fuel research, which had been in transition for some time. The Coal Board, the Gas Council, the Electricity Authority, and the several research associations (for coal utilization, coal tar, coke, the electrical and allied industries, and heating and ventilation) were conducting research with reference to the Fuel Research Station of the DSIR, but on an increasing scale, into coal, coke, coal-tar, and electricity. The Ministry of Fuel and Power was well placed to co-ordinate these efforts, and to add to its responsibility for formulating a policy for fuel supply, distribution, and use a concern with a policy for fuel research.

The new relations between government and science were most explicit where departments concerned themselves directly with the conduct of research in industry. From about 1950 the Government placed a number of substantial contracts in industry. These tended to benefit the larger firms, particularly those in the electronics and electrical engineering industries and in the aircraft industry. When defence contracting was reduced in the closing years of the decade the uneven pattern of investment in research which had been allowed to develop was exposed. At the same time the problem arose of the capacity of other departments, including the DSIR to maintain the level of investment in the modern sector while continuing to deal with the apparently intractable problem of stimulating research by the smaller firm and in the more traditional industries. Meanwhile, however, the division of functions between the executive authority and the research department within the government became more than ever a matter of emphasis.

The course taken by the CSIR * in this situation was to re-assert its special responsibility as a general research department. 'The balance of advantage' was felt to be 'in arranging for . . . scientific research . . . to be drawn together in one department, free from executive responsibilities, and seen by all to be independent of pressures of politics, or immediate expediency, and therefore able to take a detached and long-term view'. The advantage to be gained from the persistence of this arrangement was that the executive departments could then 'take their decisions by considering political, economic and other factors along with scientific advice tendered.' The DSIR had an important role to play as sponsor of research carried out in response to a wider variety of needs than those of government departments. Indeed, 'one of the main justifications of the existence of the DSIR since 1917, is that it has been able within the normal machinery of government to develop, with the advice of scientists and industrialists, a programme of interlocking research designed to meet the known or foreseeable needs of the community in so far as they cannot be provided by academic, industrial or other agencies.'[12]

The conception, expressed by the Council, of the institution's continuing value and of the appropriateness of its procedures for stimulating research, was not without difficulty in practice. Were the administrative departments, which were already undertaking research on their own account, to assume full responsibility for the activities in which they were becoming interested, the situation would, the CSIR considered, become confused. At the same time, the basic organizational alternatives would remain fundamentally unchanged. For any department moving in this direction would ultimately be in the position of obliging other departments with similar problems to come to it for research services. The alternative was for the DSIR, which was already a source of expertise and information of wide application, to take on these new responsibilities.

The consequence of this decision, however, was to highlight the basic dilemma underlying the Department's mode of operation. For if the DSIR were to re-establish its position, it would have to detach itself from researches presently being conducted which were of sufficient utility to command support from another source. Withdrawal from these commitments would provide unabsorbed capacity which would then be taken up by a renewed assault on problems of fundamental importance for the future development of

* Council for Scientific and Industrial Research; see p. 3.

industrial technology. But, in the short run, there was a time-lag between the making of a commitment to an administrative goal and its satisfaction by the bringing about of certain desired changes in organizations concerned with substantive problems. This time-lag was in part due to limitations of scientific knowledge at any particular time. It was due also to problems connected with the process of organizing for research, more specifically, with the problem of mustering essential resources from industry, the professional associations, and other bodies at various stages in their development. In attempting to formulate and execute an industrial science policy, the DSIR had to gain access to these resources. In order to do so, it had to work through a decentralized system of administrative and research organization. It had to take the indirect course of supporting research acivity without exercising full and direct control over it. In addition to the difficult task of finding scientific solutions to technical problems — itself an uncertain and usually prolonged process — it was confronted with a set of purely organizational problems. At every stage in the administrative process, it had to face pressures for directing research activity in ways which were at odds with the criteria used by bodies like the Public Accounts Committee to judge the adequacy of procedures for promoting research.

Two dimensions of such situations can be distinguished. The units which the Advisory Council proposed to set up were largely interdependent with other organizations to whose objectives their projected activities were related. Such support can be considered as *extrinsic* to the work itself. It related to the forms of organized research. Investigations considered for prosecution under the auspices of the boards and committees were dependent, to a varying degree, on outside bodies, upon whose operations their results were to have a bearing. This form of social support was of *intrinsic* value to those engaged in the practice of research. It was integrally bound up with the advancement of certain types of investigation. The former dimension concerns authority and involves the problem of legitimating a unit or units of research organization, the latter implementation or the problem of attracting contributions of resources to research projects in progress.

Institutionalization has two aspects: the actual or potential disposal of an output of results and applications, and the mobilization of financial and other resources. The growth of a concrete system of research organization can be considered as involving questions of whether, and if so, how much authority should be delegated, and of where funds could be most productively invested. The evidence which has been assembled suggests that the

findings and demonstrating applications to member firms. Twenty-three research associations submitted projects, and by 1962, grants totalling £270 000 were awarded. Smaller research associations and associations in the traditional industries were not well represented among the recipients. A system of earmarked grants was established for projects judged to be of national importance. These had an inauspicious beginning. In 1963 only one earmarked grant was made. By the end of 1964 ten such projects were being supported.

Overshadowing the Department's policy in relation to the research associations in potential significance was the decision to award development contracts to particular firms for projects which although financially unpromising were likely to lead to technical advance. Arrangements for watching over contracts were not laid down in detail. Nevertheless, at all stages, Treasury approval of expenditure was required. This probably helped to discourage industry. Of greater importance was the fact that the Government was not necessarily the user as well as the sponsor of research. There was therefore, no assurance of a production contract to follow a contract for research. Moreover, most projects which were likely to lead to results of commercial value were exploited by private firms without government assistance. An unpromising project was unlikely to become attractive to the private investor because of the availability of government support. These factors no doubt help to account for the fact that the first contract was not awarded until late 1961. Others were subsequently placed — including one for machine tools and one for computers — but by early 1964 the total value of all contracts was only £1 million with the DSIR contributing £600 000.

A certain amount of adjustment of the spheres of interest of the various bodies involved in the support of civil research for industrial purposes was achieved in the later 1950s. The Advisory Council became increasingly conscious that 'as the part played by science in national life grows and research and development becomes more complex, more organizations are concerned with the planning, execution and application of research'. One result is that 'the need for effective co-ordination becomes insistent'. In 1956 sections of the Forest Products Research Laboratory were taken over by the Timber Development Association (which had been in receipt of a grant-in-aid from the DSIR for a number of years). In the same year the ARC agreed to assume control of the Food Investigation Board's Low Temperature and Ditton Laboratories and the Pest Infestation Laboratory. From 1957 much of the formerly pioneering research of the Fuel Research Station was taken over by other bodies. A joint committee of the DSIR and the NRDC was formed in 1959 to consider proposals for the recently agreed development contracts. When earmarked grants were introduced applications were examined in co-operation with the NRDC, which was also invited to sponsor projects.

If these negotiations were to be successful and recognition of the positive role that it could play in stimulating research in neglected areas and developing new technology, to be secured, it was clearly important that the CSIR re-orient its activities independently, through the normal processes of administration. However, it was clear to many, both inside Parliament and ouside it, that measures of this kind could not provide an answer to the major issues which were beginning to pervade discussions about the requirements of a national policy for science.

The situation assessed

The post-war estimates committees seldom touched on the difficult question of priorities in research. In its enquiry of 1946-7, the committee set itself the task of assessing 'the scope and balance of the research and development programme' in the light of ' the limited resources of both money and manpower'.[21] However, its report was designed more to provide information about the existing machinery and expenditure. Nor in subsequent inquiries did they seek to determine the rate of financial return on research expenditure or to review systematically the organization for promoting and applying civil research, itself an important influence on the division of national research resources. The Government was aware of these issues. However, it was not until March 1962, when pressures of party politics added themselves to the mounting frustration of the ACSP, which was prevented by its advisory status, its restricted terms of reference, and the lack of a secretariat from dealing with broader issues, that a Treasury Committee under Sir Burke Trend, Secretary to the Cabinet, was appointed to consider the matter. The committee reviewed the scope of the civil science programme as it developed in the post-war period, and drew attention to the limited coverage, omissions, and imbalances of scientific effort and to the weaknesses of the organization for the administration of support to research. According to the Trend Committee 'the division of functions as between the various autonomous agencies and the interested Government departments is obscure'. In particular '. . . there appears to be a lack of adequate arrangements for co-ordinating the activities of the DSIR and those of other authorities concerned with promoting research and development in particular fields of industrial enterprise . . . while the division of functions between the DSIR and NRDC as regards the promotion of development contracts lacks self-evident justification'. The recommendations of the committee — that the DSIR be dissolved and replaced by three new research councils* — were the subject of much debate. Nevertheless, all were agreed with its main conclusion: that 'in the industrial field there is a clear need for greater concentration of effort, and for the institution of some means of ensuring that research is enlisted in support of those activities which are the most important for the economy as a whole'.

However, it was only after 1945 that the organization of government science began to grow in scale and to become diversified. Established administrative departments took up science. An important public corporation was formed to foster the development of inventions.

The DSIR meanwhile continued to exert influence as a body concerned with research in a wide range of fields and with varied links with a host of institutes, associations, and, towards, the end of the period, a growing number of firms. The advantage of the system was that it was sufficiently open to permit the sponsorship and conduct of research for a variety of purposes. No new scheme was likely to be prevented from gaining support through lack of a suitable agency to approach. However, while more resources and varied sources of support made for a steady evolution in response to emerging needs, the failure of the DSIR — the only institution which could give coherence and direction to the overall research effort — to re-orient its activities in response to developments elsewhere undoubtedly tended to generate confusion and untidiness. It contributed also to a certain amount of duplication and waste of effort. A major factor was conditions within the system of research organization formed by the Advisory Council, the central establishments and their clients and the organizations participating in the scheme of co-operative research. The Advisory Council was compelled to offer inducements rather than perform research itself and to rely on proposals submitted by people in the field. As the involvements of groups and individuals concerned with formulating policy at various levels exerted their characteristic 'pull', the attempts of the Advisory Council to withdraw were frustrated. This, in turn, acquired a new significance as the position of the DSIR within the administrative structure of government-

* A Science Research Council (SRC) to be responsible for postgraduate awards, a Natural Resources Research Council, and an autonomous Industrial Research and Development Authority (IRDA) to take over the remaining research stations and support for industrial research. The Labour Government, which implemented the recommendations, placed four of the laboratories under the SRC, and, in place of the IRDA, formed a new Ministry of Technology.

sponsored research and development was called into question.

The post-war transformation of the relations between government and science involved no major reorganization of the government's organization for promoting and supporting scientific research. Moreover, the major issues which were to dominate subsequent thinking about the requirements of a policy for science were only dimly perceived before 1964. Towards the latter half of the 1950s, however, new developments were initiated which did not fit easily into the established framework of financial and administrative organization. The difficulties which were encountered as a result of these attempts to assimilate new activities to older forms of organization and to reshape the latter in such a way as to leave their outlines intact began, in the next few years, to force a re-appraisal. In contrast to their important role in 1914 the scientists were deeply divided on the issues and were unable either to present a collective view about the problems and position of the DSIR or to provide a concerted response to subsequent attempts to apply central initiatives in the civil research field.

The DSIR and the universities

After 1916 attention was focused increasingly on the problem of the supply of trained research workers available for employment in industry. The more extensive conduct of applied research was seen to require a flow of individuals capable of carrying out these tasks.[1] The ability to carry out creative research, it was further realised, was dependent in part at least upon a set of communicable skills and techniques which could be acquired through formal instruction and supervised research.[2]

A scheme of grants to students and research workers was introduced in 1917. Assistance was offered to investigators working in the context of the universities and other institutions of advanced learning.

The expansion of scientific research and teaching: the pressures of democratization and industrialization

The co-operative research associations and government laboratories were relatively recent forms of organized research. As such, they were for some time regarded as the'step-children' of science, looked down upon by the scientists themselves. Since the seventeenth century, scientific research had been regarded as the personal responsibility of the investigator, doing his work in his own way, at his own pace, in a direction of his own choosing. From at least the latter half of the nineteenth century, he was often — if not usually — a member of the academy.[3]

Nevertheless, this pattern of organization began to break up almost as soon as it was formed, and shortly disappeared. Both as research organizations and training establishments, institutions of higher education were bent increasingly to meet the demands of the economy, either directly or through the action of the State. If the end of the nineteenth century saw the universities open their doors to science, the beginning of the twentieth saw the founding of Imperial College,[4] an institution conceived by its founders as the 'London Charlottenburg', and described by the Royal Commission appointed to consider the relations between the College and London University as 'founded to give the highest specialized instruction and to provide the fullest equipment for the most advanced training and research'.[5] The Applications Committee (and its successor, the Scientific Grants Committee formed in 1927) had, therefore, a not unfavourable foundation upon which to build. The response to the Advisory Council's earliest invitation was encouraging. Inquiries were made on behalf of junior staff and advanced students. Between the wars the number of maintenance allowances made available to postgraduate students increased steadily, as did the number of senior research awards conferred. The scheme remained limited in scope. In 1939 there were less than 150 of the postgraduate allowances current and many were held for only one year. The senior research awards rarely exceeded 50 or 60. £11000 was expended on capital grants for special researches and the annual cost of the programme totalled £25000.

After the Second World War, men, money, and ideas were exhanged at an accelerating rate and with growing intensity between university departments, that more modern outgrowth, the research institute, and their counterparts in private industry and government. The DSIR was drawn into the emerging nexus, and in part, contributed to its crystallization. The continued growth of a demand for trained manpower was one factor in the situation. The mounting costs of research facilities was another. A third, and less tangible, element is best summed up in the Advisory Council's guiding principle that 'provided high standards were maintained no postgraduate student should lack training, and no scientific work should suffer through lack of funds.' In 1956-7, 1000 maintenance allowances were current. Other awards increased to about 100. The total annual cost was nearly £600000. In 1958-9, 1700 maintenance allowances were current. In the following five years about 1900 studentships were awarded a year, and as they normally ran for two years, 3800 were current in 1963-4 at a cost of about £1500000. At the earlier date special research grants were given totalling £500000. The figure rose to £1750000 in 1963-4. The programme not only grew, it broadened. Responsibility was assumed for advanced course studentships (the courses recognized growing from 140 in 1957 to 334 in 1962); for administering OEEC and NATO fellowships and studentships; for the provision of grants for the purchase of special and expensive items of equipment required for particular research projects; and in the latter half of the

1950s, for such equipment even when required for general development in the fields in which projects, customarily supported by the research council, lay. In 1958 recipients of special research grants included six scientists employed in technical colleges not associated with universities. Formerly there was rarely more than one.

The universities were the institutions in which science was longest established, and with which it was associated most closely. Their role in relation to the rest of society and their own nature as organizations underwent more or less continous change in response to the need to master a refractory technological system and to meet the changing requirements of the research process itself. The body most closely concerned with these pressures, their expression in terms of public commitment to educational goals and their translation into educational practice was the University Grants Committee (UGC).[6] Student numbers rose steadily (from 55 000 in 1938 to 84 451 in 1952)[7] and the body of postgraduate students expanded at an even faster rate (omitting those taking one-year postgraduate courses in education to qualify them as teachers, from 3094 in 1938 or 6.2 per cent of the total full-time student body to 10 509 or 11.7 per cent in 1957), especially in science and technology. However, it was the period after 1945 which saw an unprecedented expansion in the universities.[7] In the decade before the war little quantitative change took place. On the eve of the return to peace there was little recruitment to the ranks of students and postgraduate numbers had dwindled. After that date the universities were opened up to selective sponsorship and advanced training and research activity were expanded under the impact of the seemingly insatiable demand of an advanced economy and a burgeoning system of public administration for new ideas and the trained manpower needed to apply them.[8]

Between 1938 and 1952 the number of full-time students of all kinds enrolled in the universities increased by 66 per cent. A greater proportion at the latter date were registered in science and technology. The expansion continued throughout the post-war period: at university entrance the increase in pure science and technology continued to be twice as great as that in the arts, and the number of postgraduate students increased as a proportion of all students. Postgraduate work loomed larger in science than in arts subjects and in pure science than in technology. In 1956-7 the proportion of higher degrees to first degrees in arts subjects was 11.8 per cent, in pure science 25.5 per cent, and in technology 17.8 per cent.[9]

A vital role in these developments was played by the DSIR, the

MRC, and institutions like them. The enlarged output of honours graduates in science and technology,[10] and the increased demand for trained research workers required the provision of extended facilities for scientific education up to graduate level. The rapid growth of the science faculties within the universities was accompanied by the growth of a demand for facilities, while scientific equipment itself became increasingly costly to provide and maintain. The research councils were, at the same time, responsible for mediating between the government, industry, and institutions of higher education and guiding the path of their growing interdependence.[11] The university as a closed community of scholars has been eclipsed in the process, and the ideal of conserving and disseminating knowledge has been replaced by one in which the emphasis is on its extension. The experience was, however, not confined to the universities. The research council too, was forced to give up a conception of itself as a body which stands outside the universities, stepping in only occasionally to provide the timely support needed for the realization of projects of genuine intellectual promise. There has, in short, been a perceptible merging of these organizations and an at least partial assimilation of the life-styles of the scientists who serve them: so much so that the universities are now more likely to have given up, than to be facing, the problem of distinguishing themselves in any absolute sense from the 'industrial research' complex.[12]

The DSIR'S limited involvement

Although expenditure on grants to academic research grew enormously in the 1950s, the leaders of the DSIR could still claim with some justification that in this field its commitments were still limited to fairly manageable proportions. Between 1956 and 1962 annual expenditure on grants to postgraduates increased nine-fold and on awards to senior research workers increased five-fold. Grants for the purchase of special items of equipment also grew at an unprecedented rate. Nevertheless, as a proportion of the total budget the contribution of the scheme to the rise in total expenditure was limited: it represented a relatively small, although growing, item in the estimates. In 1958-9 expenditure on grants in support of academic research was £1.1 million out of a total of £8.9 millions. Four years later, during which time the expansion of the programme of grants to postgraduate students recommended by the ACSP had been started,[13] it came to only £2.8 millions, while total expenditure had risen to £12 millions. The programme comprised an even smaller proportion of the universities' total expenditure. In 1960-1, it accounted for £1 710 000 out of £20 millions spent on scientific and technological research. Owing to the built-in flexibility of the programme no system of 'rolling estimates' was required to ensure its continuation under the new conditions of scientific and technological advance. It could, therefore, hardly have been considered seriously in the discussions leading up to the institution of the DSIR's five year plans in 1956 and 1959.

The attempt to improve the position of industrially-oriented research

During the period between the wars firmly entrenched conceptions — which the scientists themselves did little to destroy — held that applied science was a purely technical field of only marginal importance to the intellectual life of the universities. Advanced instruction and research in the sciences most closely related to the mechanical arts tended to be considered by university departments as peripheral to their role as centres of research and as teaching institutions. It was informed by practical, technological concerns and was the proper concern of the craftsman, technician, and engineer. Only a small proportion of the budget was taken up with researches classifiable in these terms and comparatively few persons were afforded an opportunity to register for academic courses, to undertake supervised research, and to pursue lines of original investigation of their own choosing. In engineering, no organized courses of advanced study existed anywhere before the war except at Imperial College, and even there enrolment had grown to only 332 by 1956.

In terms of the criteria normally applied by the universities to each new claim on their limited resources the potential 'productivity' of research was, as often as not, considered to be inversely related to practical motives and applied goals.[14] At the same time, the advanced research awards available from existing sources specifically for industrial research were too few to meet the growing demand for them.

Within the universities, new and promising fields of research related to industrial problems were often restricted in their development by coming prematurely into competition with established fields for university funds. An attempt was made by the DSIR to develop a flexible pattern of research activity designed to meet the scientific needs of industry through the provision of maintenance allowances (renamed studentships after the 1956 reorganization), senior research awards (fellowships), and grants for special researches. 'In the end', the Advisory Council said, 'the necessity for the State to make special provision for the supply of trained men may entirely disappear, and the natural "law" of supply and demand will operate satisfactorily'.[15] But, 'the attainment of equilibrium necessarily involves a delay which, in these times, it is essential to lessen as far as possible'.

Freedom in science and the balance of research support

Grants were made available to students in training, to a few selected younger scientists who had acquired a sound knowledge of the methods of research and had already shown a capacity for original thought, and to investigators of acknowledged standing to enable them to employ an assistant or to purchase special equipment or material. Recipients were required to submit reports at regular stages in the development of a project, and to provide the DSIR with access to any important information, discoveries or results achieved with its aid.

After 1918, holders of grants were prohibited from conducting investigations into specific problems connected with the production processes of a particular firm. In addition, financial support was provided on the basis of the acceptance of specific proposals submitted by research workers. Thus, they were limited in the range of choices open to them at various stages in their inquiries — a form of discipline which was considered indispensable if researches were to be directed toward the solution of problems of industrial importance. The distinction between the process of research and the findings of scientific inquiry is important in this context. For the administrator, definitions in terms of the latter depended on reference to a future state of affairs and were therefore unusable. He had to use information about the former as a guide to estimating the probability of producing results of one kind or another. The definition of research in terms of the investigator's relative freedom is therefore simply a statement of an assumption that those whose thought is encouraged to follow certain paths are more likely to develop ideas of greater or lesser breadth or depth.

It was the Advisory Council's belief that while it is possible for the State by means of suitable grants to individuals or the generous support of universities and other independent organizations for research to encourage the pursuit of research in pure science, it is dangerous and even fatal to organize it. Grants were assessed and made available on terms which conformed to practices built up under the education departments before 1916. Although adherence to certain minimum requirements was obligatory, assistance was provided in the form of out-and-out payments. Moreover, from the point of view of the scientist seeking support for his work, the DSIR's judgements were likely to be well-considered. In this respect, it benefited from the services of scientists of the stature of

Lord Rayleigh, Sir James Jeans, Sir William Bragg, N. Sidgwick, Sir John Cockcroft and Professors R.V. Jones, P.M.S. Blackett, Lawrence Bragg, and N.F. (now Sir Nevill) Mott.

It is doubtful whether scientists have ever been entirely free from the pressures generated by the economic and political institutions with which they are associated. Nevertheless, the tempo and style of life of the scientist underwent a marked transition following the growth in the scale and in the degree of organization of science which began in the opening decades of the present century. The independent investigator working with limited resources, at his own pace, in touch with a small group of co-workers interested in the same problems, and able to keep abreast of the literature in his own and related fields, disappeared from the world of science and learning. Indeed, long before the Second World War the laboratory became the focus of activities which were hardly known before, and the range and intensity of the scientist's influence outside the laboratory increased considerably. Scientists developed new involvements with the leaders of the polity and the economy, and after the events of 1939-45 these were more diverse and more engrossing than they had experienced in the past. For the first time, scientists were confronted with the blandishments of financial support on an increasingly grand scale. The changed expectations which accompanied such support forced upon them a general awareness of the scope of their contribution to areas of life hitherto untouched by advances in the scientific and engineering disciplines.

The phrase 'the unfettered pursuit of truth for its own sake' tended, at the same time, to lose some of its former meaning. The sentiments of those who would engage in this activity failed to carry quite the same conviction. The training and research formerly held to be necessary was predominantly aimed at the acquisition of knowledge irrespective of its applications. After 1945, the pure-applied distinction became more a matter of principle than one of substance. More and more, scientific research in the universities involved either or both kinds of motive. As the Advisory Council wisely observed: 'It may aim at the discovery of new knowledge for its own sake; or it may be prompted by industrial or social needs. It is academic only in the sense that those who work in this field obey only the spur of intellectual curiosity and should not be expected to follow the by-products of their work which is seized upon by others'.[16] A distinction must, in other words, be made between the fact of government support and the perception by aided investigators of the general implications of the terms and conditions under which it is given. Failure to maintain the distinction leads to mistaken beliefs: for example, that selective sponsorship necessarily limits the autonomy of the scientist or that freedoms normally associated with the activity of scientific research — to select problems, to publish results and the like — are inappropriate in the maintained or aided establishment. In fact, the balance of support to research performed in an academic setting may change without the scientist necessarily becoming aware that this is happening. Similarly, scientists may feel themselves to be hampered by the financial or administrative aspects of a project without developing an awareness of the changing pattern of sponsorship in the field as a whole. The fact remains, however, that professional bodies, scientific advisers to the government concerned with manpower problems, and a host of public and private groups stressing the productive and ameliorative consequences of certain types of new knowledge made increasing claims of one kind or another upon 'a part of the total services of a going intellectual concern'.[17]

The conditions governing the provision of encouragement to individual research workers cannot therefore serve as a starting-point for an analysis of the development of the respective roles of the DSIR and institutions of higher education in the organization of research with a bearing on industrial problems. Some work for government and industry was almost inevitable in view of the specialized knowledge to be found in the universities. The real issue was the extent to which this was allowed to grow to proportions which hampered them in the discharge of their primary function: teaching and the conduct of research. And whether or not this occurred depended on the Advisory Council's success in carrying out its policy of withdrawal. An inquiry into the evolution of the DSIR's involvement in the academic sphere therefore depends upon an examination of the opportunities for realizing the principle that support of training and research activities be for a limited period only. The question then becomes that of the extent of its control over the determination of criteria for when a project was likely to lead to the formation of a new department or research group within a university. For the fact remains that, despite the growth of administrative responsibilities in this field, the sums tied up were relatively small, and always stood at less than 30 per cent of the universities' own income.

The individual pattern of organized research should not be confused with the collective mode of organizing for research discussed in previous chapters. One aspect of the award system is of particular importance. While new duties were assigned to heads of departments no actual responsibility for the award and tenure of grants was delegated to them. Application for a grant was made with

from non-departmental sources. Neither were they dependent on a 'remote' agency, in a position to assess their development in financial, administrative and scientific terms.[22]

The demands of the universities for research support were not filtered upwards through a hierarchy of administrative and research positions with varying degrees of responsibility for handling aspects of what was (only for those at the top) the whole problem. It was encountered through all its stages by a committee of the sponsoring agency. It was, in addition, presented in the form of claims for new grants. Pressure from the universities came, not from aided research workers, but from new applicants for departmental support. Once granted these need never be asked for again. This was quite unlike the claims of industrial management affiliated to research associations. Whereas these implied possibly further deflection of resources to purposes other than those intended by the committee which provided them, the granting of the former involved the allocation of a fixed amount for a limited period, an event which, considered in isolation, precluded any element of uncertainty. Because it took the form of a series of discrete claims upon the DSIR'S resources it could not appear as a threat to the premises upon which the scientific grants committee's brief was based.

The break with the past which happened in 1916 lay not so much in what the Advisory Council initiated as in what it was. Unlike the UGC the Scientific Grants Committee was not obliged to refrain from interfering with the freedom of science departments and so was able to engage directly in discussions with scientists and heads of research schools. Not being limited by a fixed number of members it could co-opt the most experienced scientists in the relevant fields of research. It could, in short, subject particular projects to detailed scrutiny and assessment. Administrative relationships were not 'mediated': they did not involve collectivities or the representatives of collectivities, but rather, the DSIR as the representative of the State and an aggregate of independent research workers or loosely knit teams of scientists.[23]

From the point of view of the university authorities, the Advisory Council was a body with the aims of which they were in fundamental agreement. It was interested in the training of an increased number of research workers and the provision of assistance from an independent source to emerging lines of investigation. The programme of the DSIR enabled unpredictable, and often very expensive developments which could not be accommodated in the quinquennial budgeting system to be started at an earlier date.[24] Most of the projects for which grants were given were initiated by the universities themselves. Equipment purchased with the aid of a grant, if supplemented by regular university funds, became the property of the university or college. The prevailing lack of provision for industrial research was engendered less by restricted and short-sighted policies in educational circles than by scarcity of resources. In so far as apprehension was generated, it was connected with the impact of the programme on the system of higher education as a whole and expressed in exchanges at higher administrative levels. Discussion between the DSIR and the universities was timed to coincide with the third year of the quinquennium. This allowed the latter to include in their applications to the UGC projects from which the Advisory Council proposed to withdraw financial support and which they wished to continue. Any misgivings which they might have had were, furthermore, likely to have been either anticipated by or to have met with the ready compliance of a group of eminent scientists, themselves committed to the view that research sponsored by a government agency should be carefully chosen, limited in extent, and of short duration.

8

Conclusion

All conclusions based on documentary sources are the product of interpretation, and are open to the criticism not only that the available information is itself incomplete, but also that the writer has selected from among the facts only those which support his particular point of view. This hazard can be overcome only by attempts to weigh the relative strengths and weaknesses of facts to which importance has been attached, and others which, while significant from other points of view, have not been treated in depth. Nevertheless, while the present study is no different in this respect from others which use the same methods, the fact that the underlying perspective is perhaps more explicit and more ambitious than is customary does present special difficulties. Chief among these is that historical periods as such are only a secondary means of organizing the material. The subject of the study is the attempt to organize for industrial research; its aim, to determine the stages in which this attempt works itself out. In presenting it, every attempt has been made to describe events clearly and in the sequence in which they actually occurred. But clarity of exposition must not be sacrificed to purity in chronological matters. Thus, some events are not treated at all, while others are discussed in more than one section from different points of view. To students of administrative history the former may appear to involve grave omissions; and the latter will seem to entail the giving of unnecessary emphasis to what is already well known. The advantage which corresponds to this drawback is that events are seen as being systematically structured and as having multiple consequences.

In the introduction attention was drawn to the need for a way of seeing the process of decision-making within the DSIR which, by enabling a consistent interpretation of its activities to be made, would permit the making of generalizations. The terms used in this study have been suggested by a detailed inquiry into one particular institution. Any broader insights into the dynamics of organizations which seek to co-ordinate and promote research and development must, therefore, be tentative. General conclusions must await further research both of the kind which is possible in the case of the DSIR, and of a comparative kind. It is hoped that these studies will attempt to assess the appropriateness of the ideas adopted here in the light of detailed examination of other research councils, and of the experience of other countries where the research council 'idea' has taken root and been successfully adopted.

These limitations being admitted, we may now review the ideas about the development of organized research under government sponsorship, which have guided the research in its various stages. The key distinction is that between decisions about the control of research and decisions about the orientation of research. This distinction, and the broader contrast between the collective and the individual pattern of sponsored research which it expresses, hinges on the existence of a continuing element of resistance to scientific inquiry — of opposition to certain kinds of inquiry finding expression indirectly through the agents of a programme.

The collective pattern

The important place which the DSIR occupied in the national research and development system does not suggest these aspects of its operation. As its title implies it was the principal institution in the industrial research field. As such it had a number of important characteristics. The Advisory Council was responsible to a Committee of Council, which made possible coverage of the United Kingdom as a whole. As a permanent body, it was free from the uncertainty to which *ad hoc* committees of experts are exposed. Because responsibility was centralized in a Privy Council Committee, a single fund was provided for expenditure on research. Finally, as well as giving advice to the Committee of Council, it was entrusted with the task of supervising the allocation of resources for the support of research in the national interest. Encouragement was to be limited to strategic projects, of fundamental significance for other areas of investigation, and, at the same time, in danger of being abandoned or neglected altogether through failure to find an alternative source of support.

The formation of the DSIR expressed the desire of the Government to create a research organ of government, which would be unencumbered by executive functions and by responsibility for exploiting the scientific results which might be obtained. It was to co-ordinate and organize research and training

claims made upon the DSIR by its central laboratories and by the co-operative research associations, this fact indicates that the Department's responsibilities in the educational sphere had become incompatible with its commitments in the field of industrial research. This at least appears to have been the view of the Conservative Government in 1964. Following a suggestion made in the Trend Report, the Ministry of Science was combined with the Ministry of Education on 1 April 1964, to form a federal Department of Education and Science with a Secretary of State responsible for the research councils, including the new SRC. Industrial research and development (the subject of the proposed IRDA) and basic research and postgraduate training in fields of importance to industry, were, after almost fifty years, separated from one another.

The DSIR ceased to exist on 1 April 1964. Although it has now largely been forgotten, its considerable achievement indicates that timely and considered action can overcome inertia, opposition, and the weight of established procedure; the comparative analysis of the programmes shows not only that this is not always the case, but that such action is considerably facilitated where the tasks themselves are susceptible of solution, and the institutional arrangements which surround them are adapted to the current conditions of scientific research. Research is likely to be more effectively organized where there is a clear definition of the field of activities qualifying for support and a situation which is neither excessively centralized in relation to research performed in the government or excessively decentralized in relation to industrial research. A strong 'centre' would appear to be of importance not only in the sense of a focus of understanding, foresight, and stimulus, but also that of a source of administrative direction capable of changing, and, indeed, shifting, in response to important changes in the circumstances, and intellectual promise of current research.

The ability to maintain a clear conception of its field of interest does not depend solely on the regulatory powers at the disposal of a co-ordinating authority. If this were the case the programme of grants to students and research workers would have developed in an 'uncontrolled' fashion. Equally, a body engaged in sponsoring research will experience considerable difficulty where it attempts to combine this function with the attempt to establish and maintain, or to encourage outside interests to support large units of research organization, which remain subject to pressures of competing activities within the organizations making up the clientele or membership. The scope of the present study does not permit any hard-and-fast conclusions on this point. But the concentration of the DSIR, in terms of spending and manpower policy as well as in its ethos and the image of its purpose held by other groups and by society as a whole, upon applied research carried out for industry and by industry itself in their own co-operative research organizations, goes a long way to account for the problems which it faced and the particular course of its development. In these matters it diverged sharply from the MRC and the ARC. Possessing well-defined administrative fields they were able to survive the reorganization of 1964, and indeed, before that time, had established a record of smooth development and solid accomplishment in pioneering new fields of research and securing the incorporation of new developments into medical and agricultural practice. The underlying reasons for this are peculiar to the situation of, and the conditions confronting, the organizations themselves. In the agricultural field, the small size of productive units had caused private support for research to atrophy well before the formation of the ARC, and although the launching of a scheme of co-operative research was considered, the idea was abandoned as being unlikely to meet with success. The MRC, on the other hand, emphasized the formation of 'units' attached to leading hospitals and made arrangements for individual members of the research council's staff to work in hospitals and universities. This general pattern was necessitated by the impracticability of conducting clinical research in isolation from university teaching and hospital practice and facilities. Nevertheless, it remains true that in the absence of pressure upon publicly financed research institutes to furnish immediate results, and, more significantly, lacking anything resembling a co-operative research scheme, the MRC and the ARC were not subject to the same degree as the DSIR to the tendency for their energies to become dissipated. While there were problems of achieving a suitable balance between freedom and control in the organization of research and tensions reflecting resistance to research of a kind which research council officials have come to regard as 'normal', the MRC and the ARC were able to identify problems requiring research and to guide effectively the flow of men and resources into projects aimed at their solution.

The Advisory Council, a body enjoying considerable autonomy, came to be responsible for allocating comparatively large sums of public money among different fields of civil research. While the general field of research activity for which the DSIR was responsible was treated as a whole and financed under a unitary appropriation, the attempts made by the Advisory Council to foster the economic utilization of the results of research and to devise means for supporting science in academic institutions carried implications for industrial modernization and the development of the universities. Moreover, the organization of research in industry and the universities, independently of the DSIR, underwent considerable expansion and diversification after the Second World War. These developments made the concept of a separate field of 'scientific and industrial' research more and more unrealistic. The conduct of research in government laboratories and the allocation of resources to universities and private firms for the conduct of scientific work and training was divorced from a concern with the wider issues of economic and scientific policy. The efforts made by the Department to attract young people to careers in science and technology and to train definite numbers of specialists in particular fields over determined periods of time were, at the same time, seldom precisely co-ordinated with major developments in the field of secondary education. In considering how best to support and encourage scientific research and education it became necessary to consider the needs of industry and education as a whole, and the requirements of the community in the fields of health and welfare. In so far as the CSIR was free to make these different kinds of assessment it had, not withstanding the purely advisory status of its scientist members and whether or not they were aware of the fact, acquired the power to alter substantially the division of research effort between different national goals.

Firmer conclusions than these the present study does not permit. For ultimately the value which one attaches to a particular research council or to its efforts in different fields of research will determine what one sees in the facts concerning it. In this sense the question about the proper organization of scientific research with which the study began remains unanswered. Persons who are committed to the principle of concentrating research at various levels within the Government and in industry will continue to blame the research council for failing to overcome the difficulties which faced it. No more will the facts of its experience deter them from attempting to achieve a better balance of resources in the future. However, to insist on attributing responsibility is often to obstruct the collection and interpretation of the facts. After all, it is as much a consequence of the DSIR's success as of its failure that research was continually spilling over into institutional areas far removed from 'the pure patronage of intellectual enquiry'. Yet it is no more appropriate to describe this as a controlled development than it is to attribute it to 'loss of control'. Both terms are simply descriptive labels, neither of which are substitutes for reasoned judgements based on careful analysis of policy and procedure under conditions of loose accountability and supervision. Much that was characteristic of the

Conclusion

DSIR's operation, it has been suggested, is best understood in terms of forces which flowed from non-governmental institutions and thereby shaped its development. Demands made by the research council upon industrial institutions to adapt themselves to a culture increasingly dominated by scientific ways of thinking were strongly resisted. The DSIR was, in addition, 'open' to its environment. Central initiatives were mediated by the patterns of sponsorship through which they were expressed, and government rewards and incentives were interpreted and acted upon by scientists and manufacturers in the light of problems of conducting and organizing research in industry. An awareness both of these circumstances and of the difficulties and dilemmas which subsequently beset the Advisory Council suggests that the advantages of organizing research in a single centre rather than dispersing it among the activities and organizational units upon which it must act are situationally and historically relative. Attempts by governments to construct a science policy which allows for predictability within the limits set by the reliability of assessments of the likely path of development of knowledge in various fields will be more effective for being based on an appreciation of this fact — and on the deeper understanding that will come from further study.

Notes and references

Chapter 1

1   *DSIR* Report of a Committee of Enquiry. Cmd. 9734. HMSO (1956).
2   N.J. Vig. *Science and British Politics.* Pergamon Press (1968).
3   *Committee of Inquiry into the Organization of Civil Science.* Cmd. 2171. HMSO (1963).

Chapter 2

1   Ian Varcoe. Scientists, government and organized research: the early history of the DSIR, 1914-16. *Minerva,* 8, 192-217 (1970).
2   Dyestuffs were required for uniforms, acetone for explosives, optical glass for rangefinders, and magnetos for transport. A whole range of chemicals was involved in the preparation of drugs.
3   DSIR, 17/1. Notes on the Administration of Funds Available for Research. 13 February 1915.
4   DSIR, 17/1. *Fifth Draft Scheme for the Organization and Development of Scientific and Industrial Research.* 13 June 1915.
5   Board of Education. *Scheme for the Organization and Development of Scientific and Industrial Research.* Cmd.8005. HMSO (1915).
6   *Report of the Committee of the Privy Council for Scientific and Industrial Research for the year 1915-16.* Cmd.8336. HMSO (1916).
7   *Interim Report of the Consultative Committee on Scholarships for Higher Education.* Cd.8291. HMSO (1916).
8   DSIR, 1/1. Advisory Council minute 10. 29 September 1916.

Chapter 3

1   DSIR, 17/1. *Fifth Draft Scheme for the Organization and Development of Scientific and Industrial Research.* 13 June 1915.
2   Ed., 24/1575. *Proposals for a Scheme of Advanced Instruction and Research in Science, Technology and Commerce.* April 1915.
3   DSIR, 17/2. Selby-Bigge to McCormick. 16 June 1915.
4   Ministry of Reconstruction. *Report of the Machinery of Government Committee.* Cmd.9230. HMSO (1918).

Notes and references

Chapter 4

1   DSIR, 16/15. Memorandum of interview between A.L. Hetherington and E.B. Wedmore. 2 June 1923.
2   DSIR, 16/15. Stark to Hetherington. 31 July 1923.
3   A. Abbott. The origin and development of the research associations. *Journal of the Royal Society of Arts*, 69, 200-4 (1921).
4   General Council of the Trades Union Congress and Executive Committee of the Labour Party. 'The Future of the Research Associations' (unpublished, June 1924).
5   F. Soddy. Letter to *The Observer*, 26 September 1920.
6   Soddy Papers (Bodleian Library, Western Mss.), IV, 101, 'Public Support of Scientific Work.' Lecture to the National Union of Scientific Workers, May 1920.
7   Dyes and British textiles. *The Times*, 14 January 1919.
8   DSIR, 17/1. *Memorandum on the Proposed New Arrangements for Grants to Scientific and Professional Institutions*. Appendix 3. 6 June 1917.
9   DSIR, 17/2. Advisory Council minute 134. 19 February 1919.
10 For example, the council of the Cotton Research Association comprised 25 members, 13 of whom represented the signatories of the memorandum of association and 9 various interested employers' associations. Cotton industry: new association. *The Times*, 24 May 1919.
11 DSIR, Headquarters Library (Ministry of Technology), Research Associations, Annual Reports, *passim*.
12 H.J.W. Bliss. *Research associations and consulting work*. Paper read to the Conference of Research Associations. 12 December 1919.
13 J. Barret. *Some personal reminiscences*. Wool Industries Research Association.
14 In 1924, for example, deputations were sent to 7 provincial chambers of commerce by the Wool Research Association *(Report of the Council, 1924)*. Subsequent action included the signing by 100 industrialists of a manifesto.
15 The research associations. *Nature*, 123, 749 (1929).
16 DSIR, 1/7. Advisory Council minute 28. Appendix *(Report from the Industrial Grants Committee on Research Association Policy)*, 21 December 1932.
17 DSIR, 16/26. Industrial Grants Committee minute 47. 30 May 1933.
18 DSIR, 1/8. Advisory Council minute 69. 14 February 1934.
19 Technology Reports Centre (Orpington, Kent), memoirs, bulletins, research reports, and technical papers of the research associations.
20 In 1958, only about 5 per cent of research expenditure by private industry was on research conducted outside the firm. Of this about one-third was for co-operative investigations.

Chapter 5

1   DSIR, 17/119. Ogilvie to Curzon. 23 October 1918.
2   The Radio, Vegetable and Fish (Food Investigation Organization),

fuel (1920), Chemical (1925), Building (1928), Forest Products (1931), Pest Infestation (1947), and Fire (1947) Research Stations began in this way. The Radio Research Laboratory (1948) was originally a division of the NPL. The Road Research Laboratory (1933), Tropical Products Institute (1959) and the Laboratory of the Government Chemist (1959) were transferred from other departments.

3   Eric Hutchinson. Scientists as an inferior class. *Minerva*, 8, 396-411 (1970).
4   DSIR, 6/3. Kidd to Smith. 14 May 1934.
5   DSIR, 18/12. Wheeldon to Howgrave-Graham. 18 May 1925.
6   DSIR, 9/94. Geological Survey and Museum Staff Association. *Memorandum on Revised Scale of Salaries.* 1922.
7   DSIR, 10/32. Glazebrook to Heath. 22 January 1918.
8   DSIR, 4/64. *Building Research, Expansion of Building Research Station. Staff Requirements.* 1925.
9   DSIR, 10/57. *National Physical Laboratory Administration.* 1918.
10   DSIR, 10/32. Glazebrook to Heath. 3 February 1918.
11   DSIR, 18/13. Smith to Petavel. 20 March 1934.
12   DSIR, 8/3. Heath to H.M. Treasury. 15 August 1919.
13   DSIR, 7/3. Heath to Parmoor. 22 August 1924.
14   DSIR, 18/12. Howgrave-Graham to Wheeldon. 16 June 1925.
15   DSIR, 18/14. Tizard to Balfour. 11 January 1929.
16   DSIR, 18/4. Tizard to H.M. Treasury. 8 March 1929.
17   DSIR, 4/70. Davies to Stradling. 27 November 1924.
18   Eric Hutchinson. Scientists and civil servants: the struggle over the National Physical Laboratory in 1918. *Minerva*, 7, 373-99 (1969).

Chapter 6

1   DSIR, 3/55. *Extract from Interim Reports of Cabinet Committee on the Co-ordination of Scientific Research.* 1920.
2   DSIR, 1/2. Advisory Council minute 291. 30 June 1920.
3   DSIR, 3/55. *Memorandum on the Constitution of the New Research Boards of the Department for the Co-ordination of Government Research.* 16 June 1920.
4   R.W. Clark. *Tizard.* Methuen (1965).
5   DSIR, 3/55. Heath to Tizard. 5 May 1920.
6   DSIR, 3/55. *Note in Supplement to Memorandum laid before the Advisory Council on 16 June 1920 on Constitution of the New Research Boards of the Department for the Co-ordination of Government Research.* 30 June 1920.
7   DSIR, 3/56. Tizard to Threlfall. 10 April 1922.
8   DSIR, 1/6. Advisory Council minute 39. 30 January 1929.
9   Select Committee on Estimates. *Third Report.* Session 1946-7. HMSO (1947).
10   *First Annual Report of the Advisory Council on Scientific Policy, 1947-8.* Cmd. 7465. HMSO (1948).

11 Select Committee on Estimates. *Third Report*. Session 1946-7. HMSO (1947).
12 Select Committee on Estimates. *Sixth Special Report*. Session 1958-9. HMSO (1959).
13 Select Committee on Estimates. *Fifth Report*. Session 1957-8. HMSO (1958).
14 Committee of the Privy Council for Scientific and Industrial Research. *Annual Reports, passim*.
15 Select Committee of Estimates. *Third Report*. Session 1946-7. HMSO (1947).
16 Select Committee on Estimates. *Fifth Report*. Session 1957-8. HMSO (1958).
17 Select Committee on Estimates. *Fifth Report*. Session 1956-7. HMSO (1958).
18 *Report of the Research Council of DSIR, 1962-3. Cmd. 2027. HMSO (1963).*
19 Select Committee on Estimates. *Fifth Report*. Session 1956-7. HMSO (1958).
20 John Maddox. The right Trend? *The Guardian*, 5 November 1963.
21 Select Committee on Estimates. *Third Report. Session 1946-7. HMSO (1947).*

Chapter 7

1 *Report of the Committee of Inquiry into the Position of Natural Science in the Educational System of Great Britain*. Cd. 9011. HMSO (1918).
2 Training the young engineer. *The Times*, 10 January 1917.
3 D.S.L. Cardwell. *The Organization of Science in England*. Heinemann (1956).
4 The Imperial College of Science and Technology was founded in 1907 under Royal Charter. The Government transferred to the new College the Royal College of Science and the Royal School of Mines and provided an annual subsidy of £20000, later increased to £30000 a year. The commissioners of the 1851 Exhibition made a grant of land at South Kensington.
5 *University Education in London,* First Report of the Royal Commission, 1910. Cmd.5165. HMSO.
6 The UGC was formed in 1919 to give advice on the payment of grants by the Treasury from a single block sum voted annually by Parliament. The members were chosen, not as representatives of any particular interest, although a majority were university professors and administrators, but because they had the confidence of the Chancellor and the universities. The Royal Society made recommendations to the science subcommittee of the UGC concerning the need for development in particular fields of fundamental research.
7 Expansion of science in the universities was affected by the 1944 Education Act, which led to the reorganization of secondary education and to greater numbers going into secondary education. It

was influenced in the short-term by demobilization, and the return to civil life of large numbers of men and women whose university careers had been interrupted or postponed by six years of war. The higher birth-rate after the war led to increased pressure for admission in the 1960s. In addition to the higher number of pupils at school to the age of 17 and over (the 'bulge') a higher proportion of each age group remained at school until 17 years (the 'trend'). Between 1951 and 1957 there were increases in A-level passes in mathematics and physics of 76 per cent and 58 per cent respectively.

8   The long-term demand for trained scientific and technical manpower was formulated in fairly precise terms after the war by the Barlow Committee on scientific manpower. It calculated that by 1955 the total demand for professional scientists would be at least 90 000, but that at the current rate of university expansion the over-all supply would not exceed 64000, and recommended the doubling of the output of new graduates at the earliest possible date. The expansion in science and technology was accomplished much earlier than was contemplated by the Committee, the full target to be achieved in ten years being attained in under five. Even before this date however, it became clear that the expanded output of qualified scientists and engineers would not meet rising demands, especially for chemists, chemical engineers, electrical engineers, mechanical engineers, and physicists. This situation occurred again and again.

9   In 1962 the postgraduate numbers in the sciences were expanding at a faster rate than undergraduate numbers.

10   The output of professional scientists and technologists from all sources before the war was of the order of 5000. In 1950 the figures for all new qualifications was 8000, in 1955 it was 11 000, and by 1962 additions were being made to the stock of qualified manpower at the rate of 17 000 a year.

11   In the 1960s private industry and research associations provided universities with over £1 million annually for research purposes. In 1964-5 charities and foundations contributed £2 100 000. The research councils spent roughly £10 millions in 1963-4 (of which the DSIR's share was £3 993 000). Ten to fifteen per cent of the universities research funds were in the form of contracts from government departments in 1957-8.

12   The internal cohesion of the universities was threatened by the provision of grants from the early 1960s for relatively small items of equipment costing between £25 000 and £100 000 (see below, p. 71). Often, a condition of grant was that more than one department of a university should use service equipment; e.g. electron microscopes, which can be used for a wide range of experiments. Again, reactors were given to certain universities subject to the condition that they be used by two or more universities or colleges.

13   To involve a doubling of the total number of studentships (new and continuing) from about 1900 in 1958-9 to 3800 in 1963-4.

14   For an account of this theme in the traditions of British universities see

89

Eric Ashby. *Technology and the Academics.* Macmillan (1958).

15 *Report of the Committee of the Privy Council for Scientific and Industrial Research for the year 1926-7.* Cmd. 3007. HMSO (1927).

16 *Report of the Committee of the Privy Council for Scientific and Industrial Research for the year 1948-9.* Cmd. 8045. HMSO (1949).

17 C.V. Kidd. *American Universities and Federal Research.* Harvard University Press (1959).

18 Department of Scientific and Industrial Research, *Notes on the Grants to Research Workers and Students.* HMSO (1928).

19 DSIR, 1/1. Advisory Council minute 194. 30 June 1916.

20 University Grants Committee. *University Development, 1957-62.* HMSO (1962).

21 *Final Report of the Committee on Industry and Trade.* Cmd. 3282. HMSO (1929).

22 This is certainly true for the period before the early 1960s and for the majority of projects after that date.

23 Research groups — unlike the MRC and the ARC's research units — included temporary university employees paid for, but not employed by, the DSIR.

24 Had the UGC at any time taken over the research council's role of providing earmarked grants, an artificial cleavage between teaching and research would have been created. If applied to research in the sciences alone, internal stresses and strains within the universities would have been accentuated. University research, which is largely basic research, would moreover have been isolated from the wider field of applied R and D.

Index

academic research, 67, 72
accelerators, 80
administration, 6, 7, 10, 15, 48, 58, 77
  of support to industrial research, 26
  of central research establishments, 53
administrative history, 75
administrative staff, 19, 38, 43, 77
  salaries, 36
Admiralty, 4, 44, 45, 48
advanced course studentships, 62
advice-giving, 2, 18, 83
Advisory Council, 2, 8, 13, 15, 16, 22, 28, 35, 46, 53, 57, 59, 65, 68, 76
  members, 6, 14, 19
  terms of reference, 18
  recommendations, 20, 47
Advisory Council on Scientific Policy (ACSP), 49, 58, 64
aerodynamics, 34
Agricultural Research Council (ARC), 3, 44, 47, 57, 82
Appleton, E.V., 19
armed services, 45-6
astronomy, 19
authority, 52, 79

Balfour, Lord, 20, 40, 44
Beilby, Sir George, 14
biochemistry, 19
Blackett, P.M.S., 67
Board of Education, 10, 12, 13, 14, 16, 34

Board of Inland Revenue, 26
Board of Scientific Societies, 16
Board of Trade, 10, 26
Bragg, Lawrence, 67
Bragg, Sir William, 25, 67
British Dyes Ltd., 10, 26
British Science Guild, 11
Building Research Station, 3, 37, 38

Cabinet, 4, 12, 44, 45, 46
careers in science, 37-8, 83
Carter, C.F., 56
central research establishments, 7, 40, 47, 61, 77
  review of, 55
chemical engineering, 56
Chemical Research Board, 41
Chemical Research Station, 36
Chemical Society, 11, 12
chemistry, 9, 11, 45
chemists, 10, 11, 13, 19, 39
civil service, 35, 54, 78
Cockcroft, Sir John, 67
Committee of Civil Research, 2, 46
Committee of Inquiry into DSIR, 3
Committee of the Privy Council for Scientific and Industrial Research, 18, 20, 76
competition, 7, 25, 28, 29, 30, 32, 80
  for university funds, 65
compulsory levy, 32
computers, 57
contracts, 50, 51
control, 4, 20, 25, 26, 27, 52, 55, 68, 72

91

Index

'controls', application of, 35
  procedures, 53
  financial and administrative, 78
  short-run, 79
  concept of, 81
co-operation, 14, 15, 18, 24, 30, 32-3
co-optation, 69
co-ordinating boards, 45-7
co-ordination, 21, 44, 46, 50, 57, 58, 78
  of research associations, 33
Cotton Research Association, 27, 29
Council for Scientific and Industrial Research (CSIR), 3, 51, 58
Crewe, Lord, 16
Crookes, Sir William, 11
Crossley, A.W., 27
culture, vii, 84
Curzon, Lord, 34

decentralization, 52, 81
Department of Education and Science, 81
Department of Scientific and Industrial Research (DSIR), 1, 7, 34, 44, 50, 62, 76, 81
Development Commission, 44, 47
directors of research, 19, 36, 38, 41, 44, 53, 55
  executive responsibilities of, 43
Ditton Laboratory, 57
DSIR Act, 3
Dyke Acland, A.H., 12
Duddell, W., 14

ecology, 71
economic policy, 4, 5, 59, 83
economists, 19, 56
electrical engineering industry, 50
electrical engineers, 39
electricity, 34
electronics industry, 50
Empire Marketing Board, 40
engineering, 11, 14, 35, 42, 45, 67
  courses of advanced study, 65
  graduates, 70
engineering societies, 21
engineers, 19, 39
Estimates Committee, 2, 49, 53, 58
expenditure, 4, 14, 16, 58
  central establishments, 38, 54
  by government departments, 48
  on academic research, 64

facilities, 38-9
  cost of, 61, 64
Feilden, G.B.R., 56
fee-paid services, 41, 56
Five Year Plan, 65

Forest Products Research Laboratory, 51, 55
France, 11
freedom in science, 66
Fuel Research Station, 36, 39, 40, 50, 55, 56, 57

genetics, 71
Geological Survey and Museum, 34, 36
  Staff Association, 37
geologists, 37
geophysics, 71
Germany, 9, 12
Glazebrook, Sir Richard, 37, 39, 42
government departments, 19, 51
  links with industry, 50
  spending on research, 47
Gregory, Richard, 11

Haldane, Lord, 10, 20
  'view' of research organization, 1, 49
  committee on machinery of government, 5, 21
Hardy, Sir William, 36
Heath, Sir Frank, 19, 20, 35, 40
Heaviside layer, 45
Hopkinson, B., 14
House of Commons, 12
Hydraulics Research Station, 41

Imperial College, 15, 36, 62, 65
Imperial Trust, 17, 18
Industrial Grants Committee, 24, 26, 31, 53
industrialists, 7, 11, 26, 51, 78, 79
industrial management, 73
industrial research, 4, 5, 11, 14, 15, 19, 20
Industrial Research and Development Authority (IRDA), 5n., 59n., 81
industry, 3, 8, 9, 11, 13, 20, 21, 23, 25, 26, 35, 37, 52, 62, 77
  and research associations, 28-30, 56
  and central establishments, 40, 41
  in relation to co-ordinating boards, 45, 46

92

information, 4, 20, 45, 46, 51, 78
    in relation to co-operative research,
        28, 30
Institute of Chemistry, 14
Institute of Industry and Science, 11
institutionalization, 52
Institution of Professional Civil Ser-
    vants, 37
iron and steel industry, 23

Jackson, H., 15
Jeans, Sir James, 67
Jephcott, Sir Harry, 3
Jones, R.V., 67

Labour Party, 25
liaison, 3, 47, 49
    officers (research associations'), 30
literature (technical), 30
Lockspeiser, Sir Ben, 19
Lockyer, Sir Norman, 11
London University, 62
Lord President of the Privy Council,
    18, 31
Low Temperature Research Station,
    36, 57

machine tools industry, 56, 57
Malcolm Committee, 70
marketing, 80
mathematics, 19
McClelland, J.A., 14
McCormick, Sir William, 12, 13
Mechanical Engineering Laboratory,
    35, 55
Medical Research Council (MRC),
    3, 44, 47, 64, 82
Meldola, R., 14
metallurgists, 19, 39
metallurgy, 14, 34, 70
metrology, 35
mining, 14
Minister for Science, 5
    office of, 4
Melville, Sir Harry, 19
Ministry of Aviation, 48, 49
Ministry of Fuel and Power, 48, 49,
    50
Ministry of Technology, 59
Ministry of Transport, 3
modernization, 4, 83
Mott, Sir Nevill, 67
Moulton, Lord, 10

National Chemical Laboratory, 55, 56
National Institute for Research in
    Nuclear Science, 49
National Physical Laboratory (NPL),
    3, 40, 45
    executive committee, 34, 42
    divisions, 34, 35, 42
    recruitment, 39
    standards work, 41
    reorganization, 56
National Research Development Cor-
    poration (NRDC), 4, 48, 58, 59
National Union of Scientific Work-
    ers (NUSW), 25
Nature, 11, 31
Natural Resources Research Council,
    59n.
non-scientific activities, 5, 83
Notes on the Articles of Association,
    25

Ogilvie, F.G., 34
organization of research, 58
    in industry and the universities, 85

Paris Exhibition, 9
Pease, J.G., 11
Petavel, J.E., 39
physicists, 19, 39
physics, 11, 35, 45
    nuclear, 49, 71, 80
policy-making, 53
political pressures, 28
politics, 4, 26, 51
postgraduate students, 7, 14, 63
priorities, 2, 4, 6, 43, 49, 55, 58, 72,
    79
professional societies and trade as-
    sociations, 14-16, 26, 31, 34, 52
Public Accounts Committee, 52

Radio Research Board, 44, 45, 47
Ramsay, Sir William, 11, 13
Rayleigh, Lord, 14, 67
remuneration of scientists, 29, 35-9
research associations, 7, 23, 45, 47,
    56, 61, 73, 77
    contracts, 28
    conference, 31
    directors of research, 25
    membership, 24, 27, 30
    relations with the industries, 30
    review of, 53
    scientific employees, 29, 30